FINE DINING

The Secrets Behind the
Restaurant Industry

FINE DINING

THE SECRETS BEHIND THE RESTAURANT INDUSTRY

JACK RASMUSSEN

NEW DEGREE PRESS

FINE DINING
The Secrets Behind the Restaurant Industry
ISBN   979-8-88504-089-1 *Paperback*
           979-8-88504-720-3 *Kindle Ebook*
           979-8-88504-199-7 *Ebook*

In memory of Grandy and Granny Goose.

Special tribute to Pops, Warren Bennis, Daniel Humm, Matthew McConaughey, Ryan Seacrest, Wolfgang Puck, and my academic mentors: Steve Blank, Adlai Wertman, David Belasco, and Varun Soni.

Dedicated to the incredible hospitality of some of my hosts during the writing process: The London West Hollywood, Craig's, Bird's Nest Café (and the convenient electric car charger on W 24th Street across the street), Bestia, Bavel, Delilah, Pink Taco, Café Mak, Elephante, Felix Trattoria, Urth Caffé, Yamashiro Hollywood, Fellow, Spartina LA, Redbird, and Record Plant Recording Studios (T-Pain and Austin Mahone provided great food for thought). The nutrition and care were always splendid.

TABLE OF CONTENTS

"Jack's historical timeline uncovers the accumulation of how California Nouvelle came to be. A food archaeologists delight. *Fine Dining: The Secrets Behind the Restaurant Industry* factually describes how these outcomes produced one of the most popular cuisines in the world! This book should be required reading in all culinary-degree curriculums."

—CELEBRITY CHEF GIGI GAGGERO

"*Fine Dining* is a great application of knowledge and mindset, especially the passion and detail that goes into any high stakes pursuit. Jack does a great job blending his personal interests, background research, and application to not just restaurants, but business and life in general."

—GLENN R. FOX PHD, LECTURER OF ENTREPRENEURSHIP
LLOYD GREIF CENTER FOR ENTREPRENEURIAL STUDIES

"We all know 'Friends that eat together... stay together' and here's Jack's great collaborative example of togetherness. With a long history of cooking, passion for hospitality and the love of people, I was truly riveted to to this book. As leaders, we lead through uncharted waters, once you read *Fine Dining: The Secrets Behind the Restaurant Industry* you'll have an even better understanding, and elevated inspiration, for what we do. Enjoy and cook with your heart!"

—CHEF DUANE KELLER, JAMES BEARD FOUNDATION
CERTIFICATE RECIPIENT AND THE C.C.A.
CHEF OF THE YEAR AWARD WINNER.

"*Fine Dining: The Secrets Behind the Restaurant Industry*, tackles current topics and is relevant to our generation. In a lot of classes we learn about past success stories or strategies, but lack the relationships they have with current topics in the hospitality world. It is refreshing and eye opening to see where the Hospitality industry is heading."

—AKIO GOTO, VEGAN CHEF AT THE CUPBOARD

"In *Fine Dinning*, Rasmussen does not hesitate to tackle tough topics that continue to face the restaurant industry with gentle compassion. I was thrilled to see a section of the book dedicated to the rise of women chefs. It is interesting to look at what kept women chefs absent from professional kitchens over the years, although they have always been the soul of home kitchens everywhere. When women like Child, Waters, and Hamilton take the reins in food service, magic happens, and we need more of that."

—CHEF PERI AVARI (SIMPLY BHONU), CULINARY
CHEF INSTRUCTOR AND INDIAN FOOD SPECIALIST

"*Fine Dining* is an insightful investigation into iconic dining institutions' origins and how they were able to navigate through the pandemic. Untold stories that need to be told, so we can appreciate the true cost of food."

—TU DAVID PHU, BRAVO TOP CHEF ALUMNUS

"If you want to learn about French Cuisine, you read Escoffier. If you want to learn about submarines, you read Tom Clancy. If you want to learn about the evolution of the food business, fine dining, food trends and a revealing look at some of our great chefs, Jack Rasmussen's book *Fine Dining: The Secrets Behind the Restaurant Industry* is for you. Sit back and enjoy the ride; best served with a bottle of Malbec."

—CHEF ROC, TV PRODUCER, HOST AND
LOBSTER EATING RECORD HOLDER (19)

"*Fine Dining* covers everything from mindsets, to how Americans have adapted to many different cultures and styles to satisfy ever-changing customer desires in the food industry, which are very challenging. Trying to please the majority can be impossible, but through our diversity adaptation, America has created a bowl of amazing creativity through its culinary journey and Rasmussen highlights this in his book."

—BYRON DAVENPORT, CHEF, MBA, AND
HOST OF THE WERITO SHOW

"I found Jack Rasmussen's book to be knowledgeable, entertaining, and thoughtful. It's a fusion of technical advisement and a story that flows well together. I have witnessed restaurants fail, to the point of permanent closure, due to horrible service, even when the food was good, because no one took the time to promote positivity and service. They go hand in hand. Jack Rasmussen's writing skill, experience in the food industry, and passion for telling a story are all evident in this book."

—PAUL TASHIRO, BLOG WRITER, TELEVISION
DOCUMENTARY WRITER & CO-CREATOR, PODCASTER,
FORMER RADIO HOST, AND SUSHI CHEF

"*Fine Dining* is very well articulated and detailed, tracing the history and evolution of restaurants with informative research. Rasmussen is able to link food with health, technology and economics, and provides further insight into how restaurants placed California prominently on the Food Map of the United States. The positivity that has been expressed for the resurgence post pandemic is impressive, and the book well rounded with a lot of details."

—CHEF ADITYA JAIMINI, EXECUTIVE MEMBER - ICF,
CELEBRATED INDIAN CHEF, HEAD OF HOSPITALITY
AT DELHI INTERNATIONAL AIRPORT LIMITED, GMR

"How better to induce feelings (and learnings) than at the dining table? Restaurants are not just about food, but ultimately love, permission and pleasure; what I believe changes the world. Pleasure evokes action, and drinking Soylent ain't going to inspire change. Written in one of the hardest times ever for the culinary arts and this essential industry, Jack's book takes you from past to present to future—letting you in on the mindset of an insider like myself. Must-read for any aspiring entrepreneur, especially chefs and owners."

—LEITI HSU, THE DINING DOMINATRIX

"Fine Dining _features historical retrospective, featuring celebrated culinary icons and their influences and architecture of the industry. Peppered with personal experiences, memories and anecdotes culminating in a 'how-to' or what 'not to do' for those either already involved in or wanting to dip into this crazy, high charged, stressful yet wonderful industry. An industry fueled by amazing, tenacious people willing to redefine, reevaluate and ultimately recreate who and what we are, despite the crippling pandemic."

—CHEF JAYNE REICHERT, NBA PRIVATE CHEF
AND CULINARY EDUCATOR, SPECIALIZING
IN PLANT-BASED VEGAN CUISINE

FOREWORD: FOOD
AND MINDSET

FOOD BY BEST-SELLING AUTHOR TARA ELAINE
BRENNAN AND CELEBRITY CHEF MICHAEL MINA

Tara Elaine Brennan

- Activist, Serial Entrepreneur, Restaurant Supplier, Best-Selling Author, and Documentarian.

My entrepreneurial endeavors began by selling "Tara's Grilled Cheese Sandwiches" to the workers across the street at Vincent's Auto Body Shop in fifth grade. By 1990, I left Staten Island to attend a high school work program that put me in an NYU elevator tearing a help wanted stub off the paneled wall. I got a job at Burke & Burke Bakery in the Meatpacking District, but only after the girl initially offered the job turned it down. Joe Burke, and all, knew the college graduate stepped over a passed-out pedestrian on the steps of the interview, and her parents rejected. I didn't mind, and in fact, I liked being there.

At that first 'real' job, I presented artisanal bread to virtually every up-and-coming New York City chef of that era. I also fell in love with the brand-new electrified screech of the fax machine. Work was pursuing an opportunity in kitchens and spending time in the factory ensuring our African Bread Czar (stolen from primary competitor Eli's Bread) understood our account and chef expectations and nuances. Orders of sourdough and walnut-raisin dinner rolls rolled in all day, and I was born.

I met Michael Mina during his recognition at the James Beard House in 1992. I was responsible for the account and physically running hot bread over on foot or in a taxi was not uncommon. Custom orders and last-minute requests were typical. Jumping as high as the James Beard House staff says is unquestionable. Michael was a rising Pastry Chef out of the Culinary Institute of America, not yet known as an executive chef. My memory of that night's dinner was Michael speaking about his hometown, the Pacific Northwest. Sonoma and California were expensive and popular: Washington and Oregon were sacred parts yet exposed for their bounty and influence.

I was specifically impressed that Washington State produces 70 percent of America's apples, and I knew from my grandfather's professional fishing stories they had the nation's best salmon. When we met, Michael and I had a close mutual friend; a few years later, she had her engagement celebration at Aqua Restaurant in San Francisco. Michael and Aqua had just been recognized by the James Beard House again, this time for Michael being Rising Star Chef of the Year, 1996. In 1997, I experienced Aqua as a sales representative showing a respected chef smoked salmon and trout—but also as a bridal party guest experiencing Aqua in its newfound star position.

The years since have been vast and often magical. The Food Network simultaneously exploded on the scene, transforming America's perception of a chef. Whole Foods Market bulldozed into the mainstream American supermarket business, now its most recognized Amazon banner. Every other supermarket and supplier of fine-dining establishments shifted along the way. Costco forced quality in volume and dictates what percentage of your small business can be their account. They don't want to put family suppliers out of business simply because they don't warrant enough sales on a Saturday in Chicago. Over the past fifteen years, Wall Street banks absorbed small-town specialty distributors. Only fine-dining establishments that demand excruciating detail receive it. Banks know it's less expensive to put salmon on a truck with dishwashing fluid and bleach. COVID-19 has impacted virtually everything in fine dining, and it's a new day. Jack's book represents a fresh look at an industry that needs analysis, deserves attention, and is in a whole new world after weathering COVID-19. Chef Michael and I discuss the lasting impressions of COVID-19 and look forward to highlighting the foundational ingredients that inspire and influence trends and reality for the restaurant entrepreneur.

Chef Michael Mina

- American Celebrity Chef, Restauranteur, and Cookbook Author.

What are COVID-19's lasting effects on the fine-dining restaurant industry?

There are multiple facets to that question because you've got to break it down based on the type of restaurant. You've got fast casual, which I think will continue to thrive. So, I think you're going to see fast casual more and more because chefs have started to get into the delivery game and, for lack of a better term, fine-casual style of food.

We saw more and more chefs doing an elevated fast-casual concept during the pandemic. Almost a new category developed that's double the checkout route of fast casual. I believe experiential restaurants are what's happening next. We saw the first wave of people with multiple and usually very high-end restaurants. Restaurateurs and operators.

Then the second wave was the wave I think I fall in, and many chefs fall in, which is having multiple restaurants. And I believe we are seeing a wave now, experiential, more lifestyle restaurants: louder music, distinct lighting, night driven. These are restaurants like Zuma, the SDKs, and David Gremlins restaurants in Miami. You see these every year, even in Vegas, we're even starting to see restaurants with shows. And then you're also seeing some more private spots with some membership attached to specific venues, like Battery Club or Soho House. That is more prevalent than it was pre-pandemic.

Gawker was a perfect example of a high-end restaurant with ample, loud, low lighting. The lighting was dim, and the music was loud. And it had a buzz. And I think you know, then you saw a lot of smaller restaurants over the last decade, with a lot of chefs doing extraordinary things. I'm not saying these will ever go away. They never will. There was a relatively big trend of smaller local chefs getting little spaces and putting together a few restaurants with a more industrial feel. I think now you'll see more and more of those. We are going to see more and more restaurants that are experiential.

A lot of what we did was not only strategize ourselves and do it every day, but we'd also order from all the different chefs in town. It was good learning, where you got to see how and what the packaging that Dominique Crenn was doing. So, what's the packaging that Quince is doing? It was excellent. It was a lot of learning.

When there is the opportunity to deliver in our restaurants, we'll create a menu off our menu. Depending on the restaurant, you can pick up anywhere from 5–20 percent more revenue.

Without your people, you're not going to recover anything at all. To me, it is your employees that give you the best chance of recovering. The story continues. I plan to participate in a podcast with Jack and Tara in the Pacific Northwest, Copper River salmon fishing. Enjoy Jack's insightful book.

MINDSET BY RELIGIOUS GURU VARUN SONI AND SERIAL ENTREPRENEUR DAVID BELASCO

Doctor Varun Soni

- Dean of Religious Life at the University of Southern California (USC) and the first Hindu to serve as the chief religious or spiritual leader of an American university. He is also Vice Provost of Campus Wellness and Crisis Intervention, Adjunct Professor of Religion, and University Fellow at the Annenberg Center on Public Diplomacy.

As the dean of religious and spiritual life at USC, I've had the great honor of walking alongside thousands of university students through moments of triumph and tragedy and through times of ecstasy and agony. My students come from almost every nation in the world and embody an extraordinary diversity of identities, perspectives, beliefs, and lived experiences.

And yet, as they make their way into adulthood, they realize there is something that connects them all together and has connected everyone who has ever lived across space and time together. A simple yet profound truth—*mindset is destiny*.

We can't always control the world outside of us. We can't always get people to do what we want them to do, and events don't always transpire the way we plan. The older we get, the more we realize we don't have much control over the world outside of us. But what we do control is the world inside of us. And the way we control the world inside us is through our mindset. That's where we have real power.

To have a mindset of thriving and flourishing, we need to celebrate the things that make us human. And there's nothing more fundamental to our existence as humans than food. Not only does food nurture us physically but also spiritually by bringing us together in the community. That's why every major religious and spiritual tradition is oriented around "breaking bread." Serving food is an act of devotion, and where food itself is also a sacrament.

Today's great food innovators empower us to orient our mindsets toward creativity, adventure, and occasionally, transcendence. In an age when so many people disassociate with religion, chefs are no longer just artists in the kitchens but also mystics in the culture who expand the boundaries of time and tradition. In doing so, they challenge all of us to think (and taste) deeply about what it means to be human.

David Belasco

- Created "Taking the Leap," a popular course featuring discussions with entrepreneurs, thought leaders, and creative talent (known as one of the best courses created in higher education in the world). Received multiple Golden Apple Teaching Awards, the Peer Achievement Award for Faculty, USC-Mellon Mentoring Award, Dean's Service Award, and Greif Center Lead Blocker Award. Cofounder of the USC Performance Science Institute.

What is better than storytelling through food and entrepreneurship?

As an adjunct professor at the University of Southern California Marshall School of Business, I created a large series to explore human flourishing through the lens of entrepreneurs, artists, musicians, athletes, and philanthropists. Our course offers mental frameworks and skills on purpose, motivation, resilience, courage, vulnerability, relationships, self-talk, and how to view success and failure. Many of these same essential themes are woven throughout the stories in *Fine Dining: The Secrets Behind the Restaurant Industry.*

We all are seeking to express ourselves fully and creatively, to find meaning in what we do, to serve beyond ourselves, and to flourish in our lives. At its essence, food brings us together, fosters family and community, and allows us to share our identities and values.

As a connoisseur of inspiring interviews, entrepreneurship, and food, I hope you enjoy this book as much as I do.

INTRODUCTION

I was born into a Danish household, which means I entirely succumb to the power of "hygge."

Hygge, in Danish, means a moment of happiness and presence available with laughs, love, and, most importantly, satisfying food. Food has always been at the center of my life and in abundance.

Growing up in the twenty-first century, I enjoyed family gatherings that featured full-course meals, often starting with shrimp cocktails and ending with a choice of three pies: pumpkin, Dutch apple, and regular apple, with a side of homemade whipped cream. After school and on most summer days, I would cozy up to my grandma and compete to formulate every vertical and horizontal word in the *New York Times* crossword puzzle, snacking on popcorn, pretzels, and snap peas. My grandfather, whom I call Pops, would make me a rich chocolate milkshake with three scoops of ice cream, Hershey's chocolate syrup, and malted milk.

Every time I stayed with my grandparents, I experienced hygge the most because the food and activities were always so comforting.

These family gatherings presented grand opportunities for me to experiment with my food. I have a streak of trying the most exciting foods and flavor combinations. As a kid, I enjoyed liverwurst sandwiches, which inspired my liverwurst sandwich demo to my third-grade class. In fourth grade, I was a taco for Halloween, and in fifth grade, I was a Hamburger Helper gloveman. I would often try food groups together, like bananas on toast, peanut butter and potatoes, or tortilla chips and hummus. Like my life choices, I don't frequently enjoy experiencing much that may be conventional when eating. However, a drunken Taco Bell run at two in the morning or a Denny's dinner after a concert is welcomed wholeheartedly by me and my friends.

When COVID-19 came into all of our lives in March 2020, I went home to Los Gatos, California, from Los Angeles. This meant arriving in a familiar, diverse, and relatively high-end restaurant scene similar to that of downtown Los Angeles, Brentwood, or Santa Monica. Compared to Los Angeles, Los Gatos is less populated, and the restaurants usually rely on local regulars for service. During COVID-19, many restaurants exclusively operated with takeout food as many had to close their indoor dining.

My parents love to get takeout food. I found that all my nights became a close dinner table event with the same four people and different varieties of food each night. We'd get special rolls such as the Firecracker and Bay Bridge from Kamakura Sushi & Sake House, General Tso's Chicken and Szechuan Prawns from Mandarin Gourmet, ahi poke bowls from Pacific Catch, chicken and shrimp fajitas from Mexico Lindo, and Risotto allo Zafferano and Salmone from Centonove. The list went on. It kept growing until we could barely find any restaurants we had not been to in Los Gatos and even the more expansive South Bay. I felt so much gratitude for every meal I enjoyed in quarantine that I often took pictures of it.

When the new year hit, I created a video of several meals I ate in 2020. The list of foods I consumed was extensive, including poached salmon, Peking duck, and roasted vegetable medleys from many different well-respected restaurants. My love of food naturally led me into an interest in learning more about the story behind different restaurants. I also wanted to explore where exactly the food was coming from while understanding the crucial activities that go into opening and running a successful restaurant. Undoubtedly, tasty food will be around for hungry consumers to enjoy at their liking, but the business behind owning and operating a restaurant requires a lot more time and attention.

Some economists and business analysts believe the restaurant industry is dying or that being a restaurateur is a money pit. Many believe it is simply too hard to achieve success and only rich people with money can create successful restaurants due to their existing capital. According to a 2016 CNBC article titled "The No. 1 Thing to Consider Before Opening Up a Restaurant," about 60 percent of restaurants fail within the first year, while close to 80 percent fail in five years. *Forbes* published a 2017 article discussing restaurants with more than twenty employees, rather than small start-ups, have a higher likelihood of survival than many other businesses of the same size. There are now iterations of restaurants with more minor barriers to entry, such as food trucks or pop-up restaurants, and small, local businesses can thrive.

According to *FSR Magazine*, the restaurant industry is among the most prominent business markets in the world.

The expectation is for industry sales to reach $1.2 trillion by 2030, and the industry workforce will likely exceed seventeen million by 2030. Of course, COVID-19 impacted the survival of many restaurants by restricting sales due to nationwide control and prevention plans. But as we begin to inch closer to a post-pandemic world, the restaurant business represents a massive opportunity for more owners and food lovers to get involved within the industry. If you follow your gut and believe wholeheartedly in your mission, whether a business or a personal project, there is genuinely nothing that will stop you but you.

Of course, an aspiring owner must also understand their business model canvas, pick a prime location, understand how food works, and have a hardworking chef. A restaurateur must also keep in mind the industry thrives on successful hospitality, and most owners claim quality service drives the success of their business. Serving your customer is number one and should never be overlooked in the food industry.

I have had the privilege of dining at several top-tier restaurants in the United States and outside the US in my lifetime. I have tried all types of food, from cow's liver to Peking duck to Vietnamese red bean dessert. I have visited five-star restaurants in Puerto Vallarta, Mexico, and New Delhi, India. In Los Angeles, I have seen many elite restaurants such as Bavel, Bestia, and Dama. From ahi tuna to baba ghanoush, the diverse recipes served in California are incredible. I had the pleasure of talking to many employees and chefs over the years, getting their perspectives on their business flow and their food. Most owners seem controlled yet stressed, anticipating the crowd they feel like they must entertain. I love seeing how restaurants work and hearing their origin stories.

This book will feature several local Los Gatos businesses which closely exemplify the restaurant industry's diverse face nationwide and that have found a niche and earned a considerable following in a small town. Business, especially in the restaurant industry, is about presenting a relatable story. A marketing initiative can achieve this effective branding through marketing, the company website, the restaurant's name, or employees who embody the restaurant's motto.

This book is not very conceptual but instead outlines stories that represent what is possible in the industry and how to be successful. According to a 2021 Food Safety News article, the pandemic has affected the restaurant industry immensely, closing more than 110,000 restaurants nationwide. Despite COVID-19 closing numerous restaurants, many of them found success in being flexible and switching to mobile order, pickup, and delivery to stay afloat and continue serving the people in their communities with fresh food. This sort of innovation, and the fact that people were stuck quarantining for over a year, has led to this rise in people wanting to go out to eat more than ever before. In my town and Los Angeles, where I live most of the year, more people want to go out to restaurants now more than ever before.

It is essential to respect the food we eat, understand the history of the restaurant industry, and learn how a restaurant can become successful. It is crucial because we waste 40 percent of our edible food according to Biological Diversity, and we also have an obesity epidemic within the United States. NPR published an article in 2021 explaining that sixteen states now have obesity rates of 35 percent or higher. So not only do we as Americans need to show more gratitude for our meals, but we also need to be conscious of what we are putting into our bodies. This awareness is critical for the future stability of our country's food system, the future of our efficient citizens' healthy lives, and the restaurant industry.

How does a consumer's respect for food factor into a restaurant owner's success? A successful restaurant should be aware of their food waste as well as sourcing and stability. A grateful customer benefits a restaurant because they value the time and food they receive from a restaurant. This attitude may include positive word of mouth or a desire to thank the chef and the workers, facilitating positive reinforcement. Suppose we want the restaurant industry to thrive and stay open as omicron continues to spread worldwide. In that case, we have to place it on its righteous pedestal: an industry deserving praise, respect, and attention.

I felt compelled to write this book because I love food. Whenever I travel, my first thought is what local restaurants am I going to and where am I eating? In Danish culture, we use food to bring people together. We always overeat and have many desserts and appetizers. Food is an aspect of my life that unites people more than anything else. Every holiday, my family usually hosts potlucks, where each family member brings a dish they are good at making or can find at the store. In my family, it is ubiquitous to show you care through food, whether it be restaurant gift cards, a huge burnt almond cake, or a big package of steak from Chicago.

This book is for anyone interested in the restaurant business or entrepreneurship more broadly. It is also for people who love eating at restaurants or currently work in the restaurant industry. It will help you understand how restaurants function and everything that makes them work. I hope this book empowers readers to adopt new, higher respect for food and opens people up with gratitude to chefs and restaurant owners who work tirelessly to please their customers. I also hope this book inspires entrepreneurs interested in the food industry to take a chance on their start-up idea.

Happy Eating!

PART 1

HISTORY: HAVE A SEAT AT MY TABLE

PART 1

CHAPTER 1

THE BIRTH OF THE HISTORICAL CALIFORNIA RESTAURANT SCENE

"It's not about perfection; it's about the joy of striving."

—THOMAS KELLER

The accessibility of ingredients and the collective mindset of creating a venture has made California a prime place to curate a restaurant. Many come to Los Angeles or larger California to embrace the entrepreneurial mindset or completely reinvent themselves, and many owners have created restaurants out of circumstance rather than a clear vision.

For example, according to *Encyclopedia Britannica*, Verne Winchell came to Los Angeles with the intention of hawking used cars, then opened up a donut restaurant in Temple City to rave reviews. The McDonald brothers came to Los Angeles with dreams of pursuing careers in entertainment but then

THE BIRTH OF THE HISTORICAL CALIFORNIA RESTAURANT SCENE · 31 started selling burgers to make money. Today, we see the big yellow first initial of their last name everywhere. There have been so many successful restaurant stories that have greatly influenced the food industry today, many from persistent owners in Southern California.

Over the past century, several global restaurant chains have formed due to the business-minded savviness rooted in the state of California. The moderate weather and multiple beach landscapes the state provides, make it an ideal location for new and growing restaurants. There's also always been a beneficial mixture of culture, with many Latinos settling near the California-Mexican border and many Asian immigrants coming into Northern and Southern California city hubs.

There is almost no city in America where one can escape the famous brands of Taco Bell, Denny's, McDonald's, or IHOP. These efficient food chains and convenient classic diners originated in the West Coast state. These famous brands have even been responsible for spin-off restaurants or newer renditions. Take Taco Bell for instance: some higher-end renditions of Taco Bell include Californios in San Francisco (a cozy spot with small plates and wines), Reposado in Palo Alto (a trendy restaurant with killer margaritas), and RED O "Taste of Mexico" (a Mexican-Californian concept developed by Rick Bayless, that features a tequila lounge and patio). Thanks to this California fusion, we now enjoy tasty dishes such as fresh guacamole and chips, loaded nachos, combination plates, and the famous "Taco Tuesday" marketing campaign.

Without California, and mostly the residents of California, many restaurant industry staples and the inspiration for many fine-dining experiences today would not exist.

According to Foodtimeline.org's USA Food History site, the first colonizers of the US predominantly shaped the diet before World War II. Each state developed a cuisine based on where the first settlers were from and what they brought. For instance, in Alabama, the first settlers were Europeans from Spain in 1505. Their diet was mainly game, turkey, fish, melons, and squash. In California, what constituted the diet for natives was the natural crops that were grown around the area, such as raisins, dates, oranges, and grapes. In the seventeenth century, the missions developed in California. On September 14, 1786, two French ships landed on the coast of Monterrey, the first foreign ships to hit California's Spanish colonies, which included both Monterrey and San Diego. Due to the reference books and resources these ships carried, settlers could establish a home base of food relatively efficiently. The gardener of the vessel brought over six bushels of apple and pear kernels, as well as many bushels of seeds, pits of gooseberry, currant, grape, peach, apricot, plum, cherry, almond, melons of various kinds, artichoke, pepper, celery, chervil, several grains, and many other crops. The ship also brought potato, parsnip, carrot, radish, garlic, and beetroots.

According to the USA Food History site, the pre-Spanish Chumash, one of the first Native American groups in California, cooked all their food in steatite ollas and comics, or big hollow bowl spheres. The central piece of the group's diet was the acorn, gathered from the California live oak. Acorns were ground up and cooked as mush or turned into cake. Pine nuts, wild cherries, the cattail Typha, berries, mushrooms, and cress were all staples of the California diet too. The Chumash also prized the incredible amole or soup plant. The Chumash killed animals such as the California mule deer, coyote, and fox.

The Spanish also introduced many foods to California through Mexico. Without this introduction, many of the fine-dining establishments throughout California today may have never come to be. According to the *Oxford Encyclopedia of Food and Drink in America*, a plain diet of vegetables, fish, and game soon transformed with Mexican foods such as almonds, apples, apricots, barley, beans, cherries, chickpeas, citrons, dates, figs, lemons, lentils, nectarines, oranges, peaches, pears, plums, tomatoes, walnuts, wheat, chickens, cows, and domesticated turkey. 1769 brought the first-ever Europeans to San Diego, California. They established vineyards and began growing what would become famous California staples in almost every fine-dining establishment: avocados and sweet potatoes.

According to a 2020 article posted on History.com by Dave Roos, the first fine-dining establishment opened in America in 1837 in New York City called Delmonico. It featured extravagant private dining suites and a 1,000-bottle wine cellar. The restaurant, which remains located in its Manhattan location, is the self-proclaimed first restaurant to use tablecloths and invented the famous Delmonico steak, eggs Benedict, baked Alaska, Lobster Newburg, and Chicken á la Keene.

Tadich Grill, according to an article on oldest.org, was the first restaurant in California— established before California even became a state. The restaurant started as a coffee shop opened by Croatian immigrants Nikola Budrovich, Frano Kosta, and Antonio Gasparich. Grilled fish was also featured on the menu and was grilled over mesquite charcoal, the traditional way of cooking in Croatia. From 1900 to the 1920s, a massive migration to the United States, specifically California, from Europe, inspired a lot of culinary infusions involving German, Italian, Russian, and other European foods. The influx of people and the "mixing pot" inspired many to pursue creations and challenge the status quo within the restaurant industry.

These challenges to the status quo would be cemented in restaurant history and create staples within the industry that we all adore and love today.

According to the Restaurant Business Online Timeline created by Peter Romeo and Myra Engers Weinberg, in 1936, Robert Wein opened a hamburger stand in California. The following year, he came up with the double-decker burger and a mascot for his flourishing business: Bob's Big Boy. The next year, Victor Bergeron opened Trader Vic's in San Francisco. This innovative cocktail joint was the birthplace of cocktails with mini umbrellas, a portrait that lives within fine-dining mixology worldwide and at celeb parties. In 1941, an ambitious entrepreneur named Carl Karcher opened a hot dog stand that became the famous fast-food chain called Carl's Jr. These restaurants have inspired gourmet burger joints with their innovation and show people can sell burgers and hot dogs via a restaurant.

Not too long after that, Japan bombed Pearl Harbor, which pulled the United States into World War II. This sudden attack impacted restaurants directly because wartime rationing meant that restaurants had to be cautious about the amount of food they gave to their customers. For example, many restaurants were only allowed to use one pound of coffee for every one hundred meals and one pound of sugar for every thirty-three customers. When the war ended in 1945, the United States settled into a cautious, postwar period more focused on family and financial security. The latest invention of the television also caused many to stay home. During this period, there was a vast migration of the US population from cities to suburbs. Many people started to adopt the TV dinner, a frozen prepackaged food container heated up in the oven (Romeo and Weinberg).

Nevertheless, people still redefined the restaurant industry throughout the 1940s. In 1948, Harry Snyder and his wife, Esther, opened a homey drive-thru serving burgers and fries. He named the simple concept In-N-Out Burger. In the 1950s, the restaurants created tended to be fast-food spots because of the efficiency, price, and marketability they presented to all of America. In the 1950s, Baskin-Robbins, Burger King, and Taco Bell were all founded in California. The 1960s saw some advancements for the restaurant industry, such as the movement of the National Restaurant Association's annual conference to McCormick Place in Chicago, drawing in fifty-thousand attendees. Restaurateurs created the first food model and sanitation code with input from the National Restaurant Association, and this formalization may have led directly into the 1970s, the California Culinary Revolution (Romeo and Weinberg).

With its diversity of sweet crops and moderate climate, California seemed destined to be the restaurant metropolis it has become today. Prime crops grown in the state include grapes, almonds, walnuts, oranges, and strawberries. Amazingly, according to a Netstate article on California's economy, California produces almost all of the country's almonds, apricots, dates, figs, kiwi, nectarines, olives, pistachios, prunes, and walnuts. The state also leads the United States in the production of avocados, grapes, lemons, melons, peaches, plums, and strawberries.

Essentially, California provides a diverse set of fresh ingredients for any farm-to-table chef to thrive.

Fresh out of the American social movements of the 1960s, California chefs, food artisans, and farmers came together to create a Culinary Revolution that impacted the restaurant industry positively in many ways. One of the pioneers of this 1970s movement, Joyce Goldstein, chronicles the transformation in her book *Inside the California Food Revolution: Thirty Years That Changed Our Culinary Consciousness.* This revolution introduced daily menus, open kitchens, and influential women chefs that enabled businesses to thrive in California, setting a precedent for success for others in the country.

Goldstein incorporated almost two hundred interviews in her book, featuring change-makers in the field, including CUESA founder Sibella Kraus, Warren Weber from Star Route Farms, Steve Sullivan from Acme Bread, and Sue Conley and Peggy Smith from Cowgirl Creamery. Goldstein recalled the quote from Wallace Stegner when thinking back to how the push in California gained momentum: "Like the rest of America, California is unformed, innovative, ahistorical, hedonistic, acquisitive, and energetic—only more so." Goldstein remembered the intensity of the environment, and while most of the United States had a structure with high barriers to business entry, California was an entrepreneur's paradise.

California restaurants started to serve items on the seasonal and local menu. French Laundry and Chez Panisse were some of the first in the country to change their menu daily. Several of the chefs during the period were self-taught, learning to farm, care for animals, make cheese, and even bake bread through observation and experimentation. Goldstein proclaims of California, "We had no rules, and we had an audience to support us. It was an amazing climate. We also had the largest number of women chefs anywhere in the world."

According to the article posted on CUESA, the seasons in California are a lot longer, which presents a tremendous advantage for chefs because local ingredients are available longer, and one can almost grow whatever they desire. For example, chef Georgeanne Brennan, from Le Marché Seeds, brought in European seeds. The rise of farm-to-table and the concept of favoring sustainability and seasonality created by 1970s California Cuisine has inspired chefs worldwide to take more interest in local foods consistently. This trend includes creating relationships with specific farms and creating unique flavor combinations and ingredients rather than following traditional cultural recipes.

A *Los Angeles Times'* article titled "How California-Born Restaurants Conquered America" explains in the late 1900s, California shaped many trends we see today and has cultivated many brands familiar to worldwide eaters. In addition to the likes of Taco Bell and In-N-Out, California is the original home to Peet's Coffee (Berkeley in 1969), Round Table Pizza (Menlo Park in 1959), Togo's Sandwiches(San Jose in 1971), California Pizza Kitchen (Beverly Hills in 1985), The Cheesecake Factory (Los Angeles in 1978), Carl's Jr. (Los Angeles in 1945), Jack in the Box (San Diego in 1951), and Jamba Juice (San Luis Obispo in 1990).

Like the technological boom in the South San Francisco Bay in the 1970s that inspired the moniker 'Silicon Valley,' Southern California has experienced a significant restaurant renaissance. This game-changing movement has set a precedent for the rest of the state, country, and even the world. California has contributed dramatically to the resurgence of jobs in the global economy, and most are in the leisure and hospitality sectors. According to the 2021 *Los Angeles Times'* article "California was 'the locomotive' of US job growth in April, but it has a long way to go," Los Angeles County and Orange County added an incredible 34,600 and 23,800 jobs in April, respectively. This addition to the job market brought California to a total of more than 5.68 million jobs statewide. In addition, the leisure and hospitality sectors accounted for about 57 percent of those new jobs.

CHAPTER 2

INCORPORATE A BUSINESS MODEL CANVAS ASAP

HOW FOOD TRUCKS, POP-UPS, AND SUBSCRIPTION MENUS ARE REVOLUTIONIZING THE FOOD INDUSTRY

"Rule number one: There are no facts inside your building, so get outside."

—STEVE BLANK

It was November 17, 2021, at around 2:30 p.m., when I connected with TJ Callahan, owner and operator of Farmhouse Evanston, Farm Bar in Lakeview, and Farmheads Galley Kitchen. Callahan had something up his sleeve in 2015 when he opened Farm Bar, which he said features a menu "oriented toward a Tuesday night restaurant." What he means is the menu features straightforward decisions for a guest, featuring daily specials, a few salads, four entrées, and a few vegan entrées.

This restaurant set a record in 2021, reaching over 33 percent of their 2019 sales. Operating with a menu similar to that of a food truck, Farm Bar has become a sensation for Callahan because of his ability to innovate and see what his customers desire next. It also provides a very formal and upscale, fine-dining experience similar to what Farmhouse, now closed, provided in Evanston.

When looking at his business model, Callahan constantly thinks about what a restaurant job should look like today. He understands his business workers are of utmost importance because they are the performers and represent the brand as they interact with customers. So, pay, benefits, community involvement, and child care for his employees are top of the list. As part of his business model, Callahan gives 20 percent of his revenues to nonprofits that the customers choose. In a proper entrepreneurial mindset, he declared, "The world is changing fast, and I hope I can be agile enough to serve it."

In 2005, the Swiss business theorist Alexander Osterwalder came up with a simple yet revolutionary way to view an entire business: the business model canvas. What started in his home country of Switzerland at the University of Lausanne, with the help of his PhD mentor in Information Management systems, soon came to the United States within his company called Strategyzer. As well, according to his personal website, he is ranked number four on the Thinkers50 list of management thinkers worldwide. This tool quickly found its way to Silicon Valley, the technological center of the world and home to successful companies such as Apple, Facebook, and Google. Today, start-up companies have used his idea to become successful and dream up unique ideas that can change the world efficiently and lucratively.

One of the business thinkers most impacted by Osterwalder's idea was Steve Blank, successful founder of many start-ups and entrepreneurship professor at Stanford and the University of California Berkeley Haas School of Business. According to his website, in 2011, Blank launched the famous "Lean Launchpad" class, an iterative customer development program that fed into the revolutionary lean start-up movement, which began to define start-ups as different organizations than more giant corporations, requiring their own set of processes to flourish.

Blank created a Hacking for Defense class, which the US Department of Defense has since adopted. During the pandemic, I had the opportunity to take this class, which he called Hacking4Recovery. In this discussion-based class, companies could present to Stanford professors and Silicon Valley Venture Capitalists (VCs) interested in investing in early-stage start-ups during this week-long class.

Blank's way of teaching revolutionized how start-ups grow and prosper because it incorporates the business model canvas in an iterative, proactive state of mind. When considering a restaurant concept, an aspiring restaurateur should begin with the business model canvas and utilize Blank's customer development methodology. Blank's methodology entails "getting out of the building" and interviewing real customers to pivot the solution in the best direction possible.

THE BUSINESS MODEL CANVAS

There are four main sections to the business model canvas:

- Infrastructure
    - Key activities: food preparation, customer service, accounting, cleaning
    - Key resources: human capital (chef, servers), physical capital (pots, pans, food), finances (loans), website (online menu)
    - Key partners: food source, marketing agencies, schools, soup kitchens
- Offerings
    - Value proposition: unique type of food, name, and brand
- Customers
    - Customer segments: in-person diners, online orders
    - Distribution Channels: dine-in, restaurant delivery, mobile delivery apps (Uber Eats, Grubhub)
    - Customer relationships: get to know regulars, reward system, communicate online via email
- Finances
    - Cost structure: fixed costs (rent, licenses, salaries) and variable costs (food, utilities)
    - Revenue streams (food, merchandise, meal kits, cookbooks, gift cards)

In total, there are nine different focuses within the four overarching themes. By mapping out those critical aspects of their business, an owner can have an aggregated and organized snapshot of how their business runs, which part is doing well, or which may be lagging behind the others. For a restaurant, customers are essential because loyalty and reviews are vital to sustained business and company reputation in the restaurant industry.

BLANK'S CUSTOMER DEVELOPMENT METHODOLOGY

From personal experience receiving mentorship from Blank and taking part in his class, I have learned his methodology. Blank's methodology, the cornerstone of his lean start-up movement, takes the business model canvas to the next level. It does so by creating hypotheses in each of the nine categories and then venturing out to test each one with real customers in the early stages of business. For a restaurant, this testing phase could be in your kitchen with family and friends, or it could be a temporary pop-up restaurant or food truck that allows for efficient access to customers without investing too much capital into a full-blown restaurant.

The point of this phase is to pinpoint and better understand your customer's point of view, needs, and problems. This empathetic viewpoint will allow an owner's business and product to serve their customers better and perform better. The lean start-up model calls for scientific experimentation, validating learning, iterative product releases, and customer feedback. Because of the emphasis on feedback and pivoting, this iterative process shortens development cycles, allowing for quicker and more efficient product/market fit discovery.

Blank's discovery is a treasure to the start-up community and is recognized widely as the essential path to success in any industry.

FUTURE RESTAURATEURS

An aspiring restaurateur must start somewhere when first creating a company or restaurant. To begin, an owner must complete a minimum viable product or MVP. An MVP is the simplest form of a product one can physically conceptualize to provide the value proposition to customers. For restaurants, this can range from a simple website with the business concept to a food truck with gastronomic experimentation.

Author Eric Ries, who popularized the lean start-up movement, likened customer development to the agile development of advanced technical engineers in his books titled *The Lean Startup* and *The Startup Way*. With a minimal viable product, customer development through interviews, and experimentation is easier and more efficient because of lower costs and the flexibility to adapt to feedback. Ries also adopted Blank's customer development methodology as one of the essential pillars of the lean start-up movement.

Restaurants, especially successful ones, should incorporate this new approach to entrepreneurship and founding a vision. Especially today, with decreased access to capital due to the recession, starting with a minimum viable product could be essential to starting anew and building a solid brand. No matter what industry, technology, or hospitality, starting traditionally with a brick and mortar store has a very high barrier to entry. At the same time, lean thinking is easier to accomplish, allowing an aspiring restaurant owner to get their unique idea out there to start learning and iterating.

Due to rising rent prices and paying staff, the restaurant industry, in particular, has historically featured many barriers to entry. However, many restaurateurs are experimenting effectively with pop-ups, supper clubs, and food trucks. These options are relatively cost-effective to create, but still call for the owner to take advantage of their lessons.

Mobile cuisine is starting to make waves around the United States, especially pop-up restaurants that allow chefs to experiment with passion projects and new flavor combinations they have always wanted to test out. The pop-up craze will enable chefs to fund-raise and attract investors without putting money into a traditional restaurant. According to a 2018 survey conducted by the National Restaurant Association, a pop-up restaurant is the sixth most popular restaurant trend.

Before pop-up restaurants started to take over the restaurant industry in the 2010s, taco trucks were trendy. In 2008, famous chef Roy Choi opened up a Korean Barbecue taco truck to incredible success, causing many established restaurateurs to follow in his footsteps. This movement would only start the more significant mobile cuisine craze.

Pop-up restaurants started back in the 1960s as supper clubs but essentially went away for the most part until recently. Google searches for "pop-up restaurant" were nonexistent before 2009, but since 2014, the term has reappeared and skyrocketed with the development of the lean start-up culture in today's world. Pop-ups are usually in existing restaurants, abandoned buildings or businesses, available bars, rooftops, basements, or living spaces. In New York, San Francisco, and Chicago, entire malls provide space for successful pop-up restaurants. Food delivery services like DoorDash, Uber Eats, and Postmates have entered the pop-up realm by experimenting with kitchen trailers and renting out rooms for new concept testing.

The pop-up trend is not likely to die anytime soon because it allows new chefs and established chefs alike to avoid enormous expenses for their new unique visions and concepts.

According to a 2021 article by Emily Wimpsett posted on *QSR Automations*, some highly successful pop-up restaurants in the United States include Nashville's Otaku Ramen, San Francisco's Lazy Bear, and New York City's Superiority Burger. Otaku Ramen was the country music city's first-ever ramen joint, and it was a smash hit. Owner Sarah Gavigan utilized locally sourced pork bones to create a delicious broth with her noodles and braised pork. Lazy Bear only sells tickets every third Monday of the month for the next month to get the chance for an interactive dining experience, where you chat with the chefs in the kitchen after eating. Superiority Burger is NYC chef Brook Headley's healthy spin on a burger joint, offering savory vegetarian options and classic meat lover plates. These spots have earned popularity fast, often empowered by the chef and owner's experimental passion.

In 2020, according to a *Restaurant Business* article by Peter Romeo, bars and restaurants dropped in sales by 19.2 percent. The industry finished 2020 with $659 billion in sales, though it was forecast before the pandemic began to end with just shy of $900 billion in sales. However, taking a closer look, full-service, sit-down restaurants were down 34 percent while fast-food restaurants were down only 7 percent. For full-service restaurants to alleviate their tiny profit margin, especially after being hit with COVID-19, business models had to incorporate a food delivery channel within their model through companies like Uber Eats and DoorDash.

But full-service restaurants only make a 30 percent commission from this delivery model, which means they would be operating at a loss if their business model shifted toward delivery.

The demand for drive-thru and easily accessible restaurants, such as food trucks, has grown immensely over the last year.

Many people have adopted takeout as a routine over sit-down eating. According to an article posted by PR Newswire, a whopping 68 percent of consumers are more likely to buy takeout than before the pandemic. In addition, 53 percent of consumers go as far as to say takeout and delivery are essential to their lifestyles.

For full-service restaurants to remain above water, they will need to look into multiple revenue streams. Some of these options include:

- Meal Kits
- Subscription menus
- Selling Grocery Items

Meal Kits: One option for restaurateurs could be meal kits, or a packaged set of ingredients with a recipe to follow, allowing customers to cook it in their own homes. Restaurants specifically have a favorable available market in this arena because of the uniqueness and quality vision of the chef.

Subscription menus: These have also been a prevalent trend in the restaurant industry to guarantee restaurants a steady cash flow stream. This new method is a modern setup. The customer pays for a daily, weekly, or monthly subscription, enabling them to pick up menu items and beverages from a restaurant frequently and on their own time. In a 2020 article posted by Sam Bloch of The Counter explains, "Industry experts, restaurant owners, and entrepreneurs are bullish on restaurant subscriptions—a business model where, for a fee ranging from a few bucks a month to over a thousand for the year, customers receive discounted or unlimited menu items."

Selling grocery items: According to CNN Business, this also presents a fantastic opportunity for restaurant owners. During the pandemic, many restaurateurs pursued this business deal to be categorized as "essential businesses" when dining had to close down. Even though grocery items have significantly low business margins, restaurants have an advantage because they can source their inventory directly and cross-sell products with different things. This savvy strategy allows restaurateurs to control their margins more because they are not held down to the traditional high-volume, low-margin model.

Incorporating any of these three strategies into the business model will allow restaurants to recover from the pandemic by utilizing physical space without forcing or relying solely on delivery. With the transition, many dine-in restaurants are going through to adapt their business model powerfully, and many apps have emerged to help. Tock enables restaurants to take advantage of meal kits, Table 22 allows owners to incorporate subscription menus, and Spud and Good Eggs are beneficial eGrocery platforms based in Canada and California. Although there is a fee with every app, the owner gains access to new audiences, and the payoff balances out.

Ultimately, a business model canvas is essential for any business, especially a start-up that needs consistency and efficiency while remaining above water financially. Restaurants in the start-up industry have to be innovative when thinking about their cost-benefit analysis. Especially in a post-2020 world, innovative business models such as food trucks, pop-ups, and subscription menus are very attractive concepts. Owners should consider this when opening a new restaurant or spreading their idea to new cities.

There are multiple aspects of a business to consider when starting a company and the business model canvas reminds us of this. It may be great to have an incredible concept or idea that is unique to the world, but to become a full-fledged business concept that runs well and also makes a profit, you must consider all nine concepts of the canvas:

- Value proposition
- Key partners
- Key activities
- Key resources
- Customer relationships
- Distribution channels
- Customer segments
- Cost structure
- Revenue streams

When considered and developed thoroughly with all nine concepts, the business has a much higher chance of succeeding.

For a restaurant, thinking about the food and menu matter, along with the paths of distribution. These are essential elements for creating a model that works, along with customer relationships and cost structure. That is why food trucks, pop-ups, and subscription models have become more and more popular today. As long as you give each piece of the puzzle some thought, give it a shot.

Success may be right around the corner, and if not, failure will provide a powerful lesson for your next shot.

CHAPTER 3

HISTORY OF LARGE CHANGES IN THE INDUSTRY

"Brilliant thinking is rare, but courage is in even shorter supply than genius."

—PETER THIEL

My family loves to eat out even on the weekdays, and we make a celebration out of it each time. Whether it is the local Mexican cantina, Pedro's (where I had my surprise eighteenth birthday), or the Italian restaurant down the street called Willow Street (it has our favorite whole wheat bread with olive oil and balsamic). Fine dining has transformed and taken on a life of its own, as more people can afford a night out and love to get together over food that is aesthetically pleasing and leaves us more satisfied than if we'd had a lovingly home-cooked meal.

"Fine dining" is a vague term used to encapsulate the vision many owners had to transform the act of eating into an art form. According to *The History of Fine Dining: Modern* by Guillermo Valencia, as culinary art started to become more refined and in tune with French culture, A. Boulanger opened his very first business that offered soups and broths. That is how the very first restaurant came to be. The company was named Restorative or "Restaurant" because it denoted the nutritious quality of food, helping customers restore themselves with each bite.

In 1782, the first luxury restaurant was opened in Paris called La Grande Taverne de Londres, by Antonio Beauvilliers. This talented man also wrote a book published in 1814 titled *The Art of Cuisine*. Through this book, more people became aware of fine dining. It also brought the famed chef more popularity, reinforcing the up-and-coming fine-dining scene. Brilliant-Savarin, a famous gastronomic chronicler, credited Beauvilliers, in an online *Food Reference* article, with being the first man to combine the four essentials of a dining room: "an elegant room, smart waiters, a choice cellar, and superior cooking."

At the end of the 1700s, the French Revolution caused many to have the opportunity to eat out by leveling the playing field socially while reducing the number of households with culinary establishments, as both the upward moving middle class and the falling aristocracy grew closer together. The leveling of these two seemingly separate classes gave birth to several fine-dining establishments. Marie Antoine Caréme, a superstar of the French culinary world, became the first celebrity chef. He was best known for his extreme attention to detail in every dish he created. This fine-dining experience was further developed in the nineteenth century by wealthy aristocrats in Europe and well-off Americans. During the nineteenth century, the Paris restaurant scene continued to rise, and after the defeat of Napoléon, many Europeans flocked to Paris for gourmet food. By the end of the nineteenth century, advancements in transportation made luxury tourism a vast industry and eating while traveling became a proper art form (*The History of Fine Dining: Modern*).

Throughout the twentieth century, restaurants continued to transform through world wars. During World War I, many Americans living abroad in Paris returned to the United States to foster café culture. In Washington, DC, the fact that wartime bureaucracy required more workers increased the ranks of many working women while also increasing the number of women customers. This transformation caused many restaurants to install female bathrooms. Due to the draft that started in 1917, there was an apparent shortage in labor staff as foreign immigration ceased. Serving in restaurants became female-dominated overnight. White women replaced immigrants who settled in rural places. Military members became accustomed to the American diet of beef and potatoes, bread, and milk. Wartime stimulated a more businesslike attitude because businesses had to work extra hard to profit. The following decade saw the rise of sandwiches, salads, milk, and soft drinks rather than the heavy and meaty meals presented the decade before. War plants in Southern California that lacked any housekeeping facilities caused a massive influx of over 250,000 workers to start eating at public restaurants (*The History of Fine Dining: Modern*).

During World War II, lobster, pizza, seafood, and Polynesian food became popular on menus. TV dinners became extremely popular because the military had to turn to them to feed their soldiers, so the restaurant industry turned to frozen foods rather than entirely based on processed and fresh foods during this time. A few foods became staples in the restaurant industry, specifically fries and cheesecake. The air freight industry, developed during the war, allowed restaurants to ship food from all over the world to their particular restaurants due to several available pilots and aircraft. America was known, up until the 1900s, for horrible food choices high in grease and poor in table manners. America started to transform once it began introducing more unique foods from Europe. For example, Henri Soule introduced America to French fare at the 1939 World's Fair, which served as the cornerstone of America's haute cuisine. Le Pavillon served as a prime example for many other restaurants trying to perfect formal and elaborate service. At Le Pavillon, royalty, socialites, and celebrities were seated at an exclusive area called "the blueblood station" (*The History of Fine Dining: Modern*).

Transportation in the United States was a significant catalyst for the rise of the restaurant industry in the United States. In the nineteenth century, the invention of railways and steamships meant that more people could travel, which meant that the demand for restaurants increased steadily. Inspired by the fine-dining industry in Paris, dining in the United States and throughout Europe grew closer to what we think of dining out today: private tables, choosing from an à la carte menu, and paying for the check at the very end of the meal. Before this, restaurants operated mostly locally, serving the hometown crowd. The rise of the transportation industry made the restaurant industry more visible nationally and internationally, allowing people to try local favorites across the country (*The History of Fine Dining: Modern*).

In the early twentieth century, many restaurant owners wanted to develop a memorable brand. This desire led to the rising popularity of franchise restaurants, coupled with the public's heightened awareness of germs. It contributed to the success of two restaurants with all-white interiors: White Castle and White Tower. These restaurants had a mission to prepare food in a safe, sterile, modern environment, and the emergence of many other fast-food brands soon followed. Arguably, the most considerable development in this movement was the rise of the fast-food giant McDonald's. Incredibly, the fast-food company started as a hot dog stand but switched to hamburgers in 1948. Inspired by Henry Ford's assembly line concept, the brothers and cofounders delivered the fastest and cheapest food possible by employing low-skilled workers. Ray Kroc, a salesman, saw the infinite potential of McDonald's and bought out the restaurant in 1954 (*The History of Fine Dining: Modern*).

In the 1950s, there was a rapid growth of fast food, while the 1960s introduced more chain businesses and monopolies in the industry. The McDonald's formula for franchising changed American dining forever. Throughout the 1950s and 1960s, many more franchise restaurants started to flourish, and interestingly, they were not necessarily "American" food concepts. Brands such as Taco Bell (Mexican cuisine), Kentucky Fried Chicken (inspired by Scottish and West African cuisine), and Pizza Hut (Italian) were some of the first franchises to become successful in the United States. Pizza became an essential American staple during the mid-1900s and featured in several chains such as Domino's, Little Caesars, and Papa John's. In later decades, more families started to eat out due to their busy nine to five working schedules, which shortened their bandwidth to prepare meals and allowed them to pay for restaurant dinners. This newly created phenomenon inspired cheap family style restaurants such as *Olive Garden, BJ's,* and *Applebee's (The History of Fine Dining: Modern).*

One could describe the 1970s and 1980s as a food renaissance in America because of the increase in fine-dining restaurants where the general public had access to eat. Artists who usually rented studio apartments to paint or write a book were trying to become chefs and cooking up masterful concoctions. The focus on food became highly apparent during the late years of this century. This focus inspired many to open restaurants or explore different culinary foods from other parts of the world. Movie scenes and television shows featured restaurants.

The comedic sitcom of the 1990s, called *Friends,* was famous for having a specifically designed set as a coffee shop. The coffee shop was called Central Perk in the show and has become a renowned portrait of what coffee shops could be during the 1900s. Many essential scenes in extremely memorable movies got their inspiration from the restaurant industry and the rise of fine dining. The restaurant industry became an industry where businesses could flourish as the rise of customers led to a comprehensive obtainable marketplace.

A restaurant was a staple in popular culture and business like never before.

FOOD AND ECONOMICS

The massive recession in 2008 caused many casual chains like *Applebee's* to take a significant income hit as many people had to turn to cheaper food to survive economically. Unemployment rates hit 10 percent, and many lost their businesses for which they had worked their whole lives. According to the *Time* article, "Restaurants Face Lean Times in the Economic Downturn" by Jeremy Caplan, it caused the restaurant industry to suffer completely stagnant sales for the first time in two decades. This stagnation made it extremely difficult for chains and independent eateries to upgrade equipment and hire quality staff.

Hudson Riehle, an economist and senior vice president for the National Restaurant Association's Research and Knowledge Group, declared 2018 the most challenging year for restaurants since 1991 in a January 2021 *Nation's Restaurant News* article. But, after the 2008 stock market crash, the restaurant industry has been in an upswing. The fast-casual space, including restaurants such as Panera Bread, was overgrowing within the restaurant industry because of the waiter-free brand identity.

According to Statista studies, "US: Annual Unemployment Rate 1990–2018" and "Total US Retail and Food Services Sales 2020," unemployment rates hit a low of 3.7 percent in 2019 while total food sales increased steadily since 2017, with retail and food services sales reaching 6.22 trillion dollars in 2020. The National Restaurant Association recorded that as of 2017, there were over one million restaurant locations in the United States which employ 14.7 million people in the field.

COVID-19 did have a drastic effect on the industry, as seen by the huge jump in the unemployment rate from 2019 to 2020 recorded by the same Statista articles. The jump went from 3.7 percent to 8.1 percent. In 2021, however, due to restaurants figuring out more ways to cope with their troubles and the government helping to alleviate some problems with stimulus packages, the rate went down to 5.3 percent in 2021.

FOOD AND HEALTH

Since the beginning of the restaurant industry, there has also been an increase in the demand for organic products. According to the Organic Trade Association, the need for organic products has increased every year since the 1990s. From 2008 to 2015, total US organic sales and growth increased from $20 billion to $40 billion. Incredibly, America was spending nearly $50 billion on organic products each year, and over 82 percent of households were buying it, many for reasons such as health, the environment, and quality taste.

Healthy restaurants have had an extremely positive impact on the health of Americans because they have put healthy and nutritious ingredients on a very firm pedestal. However, due to the increase in obesity, there has been a strong move since the 1980s to serve healthier food. No longer are there exclusively foods with high fat and high sodium on menus. However, most eateries have low-calorie, vegetarian and gluten-free options.

Because of COVID-19, most restaurants can no longer support a buffet-style lunch with an all-you-can-eat option, which has indirectly led to a reduction in portions due to fewer self-serving portions. More menu labeling also exists, spotlighting ingredients within a dish, sometimes even offering a calorie count next to each plate. For example, one of my family's favorite Italian chain restaurants called The Old Spaghetti Factory, founded in 1969, provides the calories for each dish it serves on its menu.

FOOD, TECH, AND MEDIA

American chefs are now national celebrities, such as Bobby Flay, Thomas Keller, José Andres, Suzanne Goin, Rick Bayless, and Grant Achatz. The increase in their profiles is thanks to the rise of the Food Network. It is hard to imagine a world without Guy Fieri visiting the best diners across the country or even *Chopped* contestants scrambling to get their plates finished.

The man who dreamed up the vision behind the Food Network was Reese Schonfeld, cofounder of CNN. Schonfeld, who did not even have a kitchen in his household, chose to take a big gamble on the first-ever food-focused network. According to *Grub Street's* "How Food Network Turned Big-city Chef Culture into Middle-America Pop Culture," the show's first-ever food celebrity, Sara Moulton, was hugely skeptical at first. She had a horrible on-set experience, and her on-air kitchen did not even have an oven.

Allen Salkin, the author of *The Uncensored History of the Food Network*, acknowledged in his book that it is tough to cook on camera, and many end up cutting themselves. His book has a new afterword featured on Amazon, and the selling page features a very telling quote from Martha Stewart: "I don't want this shown. I want the tapes of this whole series destroyed." Despite or maybe thanks to the mediocre beginnings, the Food Network took off. Guy Fieri, Giada De Laurentiis, Bobby Flay, Ina Garten, and Valerie Bertinelli are just some of the many stars who have made a living from displaying their cooking or tasting skills for America to see.

According to a 2015 article by Monica Burton posted on Eater, the #MeToo movement also found its way into the restaurant industry. Celebrity chef Mario Batali, and other restaurateurs like Josh Besh and Ken Friedman, were accused of mistreatment in the workplace. Women started to have louder voices within the restaurant industry, and many were making a difference by making their restaurant concepts come to life. OpenTable CEO Christa Quarles started an Open Conversation dinner series strictly dedicated to women within the food industry. The positive trend within the industry was the increase of spotlighting authentic workplace culture and allowing women to have a more significant presence in the discussion.

Social media has enabled the rise of celebrity chefs and the entry of restaurant workers into the #MeToo movement as well. Likewise, it's had a significant impact on the industry in general. The rise of social media has dramatically impacted how we consume food today.

According to a Pew Research study titled "10 Facts About Americans and Facebook," in 2018, 68 percent of Americans used Facebook, 35 percent of Americans used Instagram, and 24 percent of Americans had a Twitter account. The utilization of funds for posting food is absurdly high and given the fact that the average person has three accounts, it means the circulation is hitting an all-time high. The foodie craze altered the way we eat our food, following where people take us and what people eat every day to stay on top of what is popular.

To keep up with the social media-obsessed society, you have to visit trendy restaurants present on social media.

Also, food is available whenever we want it. Incredibly, Amazon Prime will deliver food to you in two days, so you do not have to do the grocery run yourself. There also now exists a vast number of restaurants that bridge the gap between fast food and fine dining to take advantage of the high-quality food Americans love while also tapping into the convenience and efficiency aspects that impatient Americans also love.

Restaurants such as Panera Bread, Shake Shack, and Moe's Southwest Grill have all taken advantage of this fine and fast model that took off after the 2008 recession. According to a *Restaurant Business* blog post, fast-casual chains grew sales by 8.9 percent in 2017. The attraction to places like Chipotle, Subway, and Starbucks was the ability to enjoy an occasion with friends without having to dress up for a fancy five-star restaurant.

It is no secret that enjoying restaurant food from your house has become incredibly more accessible too. Delivery services such as Grubhub, Postmates, Uber Eats, and Slice have become mainstream mobile applications dedicated to delivering restaurant food to people's current locations. According to a 2021 Pew Research study called "Mobile Fact Sheet," the number of people who own phones has increased from 22 percent in 2008 to over 77 percent today. On their online website, CNBC has forecast a 79 percent surge in total US food home delivery over five years, rising from 2017's $43 billion to $76 billion by 2022. This at-home trend has even increased the diversity of cuisine ordered. What used to be exclusively to-go Chinese food or pizza has turned into bagels, Indian food, Mediterranean food, and so much more.

Undoubtedly, the attention we place on food in our culture today is magnificent. It has not only become part of fine dining, but also popular culture. According to a Pew Research article titled, "Public Views about Americans' Eating Habits," the most significant majority of people focus on the "taste sensations of every meal" more than any other aspect. As

Americans, we have become obsessed with fine dining, dramatizing our nights in the town, and enjoying every bite of a three-course meal presented as if it fits in an art museum in the UK.

So, go big or go home. With food today, there is no other option but to go big.

CHAPTER 4

FARM-TO-TABLE

"Agriculture is a fundamental source of national prosperity."

—J.J. MAPES

The *New York Times* defined the Californian food movement as "California Cuisine" in 1982 after many chefs pushed for it. Marian Burros, a famous *New York Times* food columnist, defined the cuisine with wild imagery in a 1982 *New York Times* food column. Marian Burros coined the term "California Cuisine" to describe California's farm-to-table movement. She defined the cuisine with wild imagery while acknowledging that the cornerstone would always be the freshness of ingredients.

A farm-to-table diet means using locally sourced ingredients from farmers. Cooks prepare the food, which is often very seasonal. As well, chefs garnish the plate with vegetables, replace red meat with chicken and fish, prefer grilled over fried, value ethnic ingredients, aim for simplicity in presentation, and sometimes combine foods in a very unique and sophisticated fusion.

California Cuisine is unique because of the autonomy it gives the chef. Because of sourcing the food locally, chefs have powerful control over what they want to bring into their kitchen and how they want to express their creativity within their food. This empowering freedom united innovative chefs to collaborate closely with farmers, winemakers, breeders, dairymen, and even cheese makers. California and this farm-to-table movement inspired the rise in organic farming and the Farmers Market. This incorporation of the direct growing of ingredients to the cooking process in California inspired cooking to be part of social life. Eating and drinking publicly in restaurants became normalized as an art form.

According to a *Food Timeline Blog* posted by Lynne Olver titled "American Presidents' Food Favorites," Ronald Regan hosted Queen Elizabeth in California, rather than Washington, DC, to feed her the best food in America in 1983. Regan's social secretary described the dinner as a "toast to the Cuisine of California." The delicious meal featured a lamb and lentil salad in raspberry vinegar and walnut oil dressing, as well as salmon poached in Zinfandel, a California-grown, red wine.

When thinking of this flourishing California invention of farm-to-table cuisine, there are three chefs that have contributed and have spotlight attention for their excellent achievements in the field: Jeremiah Tower, Alice Waters, and Wolfgang Puck.

JEREMIAH TOWER

Chef Jeremiah Tower is one of the many names credited with California's incredible influence on the food industry. Known for his creativity in defying the regular rules of the restaurant industry, Tower worked at Chez Panisse in Berkeley, California, in the 1970s. In the 1980s, Tower opened Stars restaurant, a critically acclaimed city hotspot. In *The Last Magnificent*, a documentary about Tower, Anthony Bourdain said: "Jeremiah changed the world of restaurants and restaurant cooking. His menus made a complete reevaluation of not just American food and ingredients—but food." Tower published his tenth book in 2018 titled *Flavors of Taste: Recipes, Memories and Menus*. In this book, he shares seventy-five childhood recipes supplemented with photography and nostalgic stories. He even includes the meals he prepared for Elizabeth David in England, Elizabeth Taylor in San Francisco, and Sophia Loren.

According to the *Portland Mercury's* article by Andrea Damewood and colleagues, "The Untold Story of Jeremiah Tower," Tower grew up in a family household that perpetuated neglect due to his abusive and alcoholic parents. He recounted memories of his mother being too drunk at fancy hotel parties to even cook a meal, which forced him to bring together the ingredients. In 1972, when Tower entered the Chez Panisse, owner Alice Waters hired him on the spot. What impressed Waters about Tower was his attention to detail and passion for the food industry, unlike no other. Tower's time at Chez Panisse was crucial to his development as one of the next big chefs in the world.

After that, he wanted to create his own concept, which is when Stars was born. Stars, open from 1984 to 1999, was known for its lavish and busy open kitchen and was considered one of the birthplaces of California Cuisine, New American Cuisine, and the concept of a "celebrity chef." Because of its popularity, Stars was one of the top-grossing restaurants in the United States. Towers opened a branch in Napa Valley, Palo Alto, Manila, and Singapore (Damewood et al.).

In regard to the media, Tower attends food festivals and has television experience. However, he says his features on television were embarrassing, as Bourdain had a microphone on him at all times. He would often forget about the microphone and say the most outrageous things. When he saw the documentary premiere at the Tribeca Film Festival, showing people residing in New York the revolution that happened on the other side of the country, Tower said he thought it would be a great example for young chefs of the highs and lows in the restaurant industry. He tried to let it all hang out, allowing the audience to see the stupidity as well as the celebratory occasions.

Tower also attended the Hawaii Food and Wine Festival, where he had the opportunity to get involved and showcase his culinary fusion skills. Tower was excited to be reunited with fellow chef Roy Yamaguchi and meet more exceptional chefs on the islands that have been influenced by the farm-to-table formula, serving fresh fish and incorporating delicious pineapple, coconut, and macadamia nuts within their recipes.

ALICE WATERS

In her contribution to Britannica, Melissa Albert credits Berkeley, California, or even more specifically, Chez Panisse, as an all-star home to many important players in the food industry. The owner of the establishment, Alice

Waters, opened it in 1971 and, little to her knowledge then, shepherded a global movement to use the highest quality ingredients that are sourced locally and served according to the seasons.

Waters graduated from the University of California, Berkeley in 1967 with a degree in French Cultural Studies. After realizing her interest in food, she worked at Montessori School in London and had a seminal year traveling and experiencing the cuisine throughout France. When she boldly opened Chez Panisse in 1971, she wanted to create a sophisticated concept that appreciated the food being grown around her. She created a five-course, prix fixe (set to a fixed price) menu that changed on a daily basis. This revolutionary concept remains the cornerstone of her restaurant, which prides itself on following the seasons and only serving the freshest Californian ingredients (Britannica, Albert).

In 1980, she opened an upstairs café featuring an à la carte menu. Because of her concept, she developed close relationships with farmers and ranchers who enjoyed supplying her restaurant with their best produce and meat. Then, Waters opened Café Fanny in 1984, a stand-up café with both breakfast and lunch options. Similar to her former colleague Tower, Waters shared her wisdom in many books throughout her career. Some of her most famous books include *The Chez Panisse Menu* Cookbook, *Fanny at Chez Panisse*, and *Chez Panisse Vegetables*. She received the prestigious Humanitarian of the Year Award from the James Beard Foundation, has been named the best chef in America many times, and earned an honorary degree from Mills College in Oakland, California (Britannica, Albert).

Today, Waters is working with Martin Luther King Junior High School in Berkeley to develop a cutting-edge food-based curriculum. This incredible initiative serves to teach the farm-to-table process that Waters trailblazed herself over fifty years ago. Her project involves students in the gardening, harvesting, cooking, and eating processes to ingrain in them much-needed respect for themselves, the food they eat, and the planet around them at a young age. This school in Berkeley is currently being used as a pilot to serve as a model for many more schools across the country (Britannica, Albert).

Alice also has a hand in the Horticulture Project at the San Francisco County Jail, which teaches organic gardening to prisoners as a way to heal their confidence and teach them values of respecting the planet and positive community involvement (Britannica, Albert).

WOLFGANG PUCK

The California movement would not be complete without the legendary influence of Wolfgang Puck, who broke barriers in the normal traditions of French cuisine and Nouvelle cuisine (eclectic international cuisine). According to a blog by the Wine History Project of San Luis Obispo, posted by Libbie Agran, Puck came to the United States in 1973 from his home country of Austria. He had an apprenticeship in France at Maxim's in Paris and L'Hotel de Paris in Monaco. When the young chef arrived in America, he worked in Indiana before coming to Los Angeles to work at Ma Maison, Patrick Terrail's Nouvelle Cuisine restaurant.

While in the Entertainment Capital of the World, Puck experimented with flavors from different cultures. He has a drive to genuinely represent California Cuisine as a reflection of the rich ethnic diversity in Southern California. With this in mind, he opened Spago on the Sunset Strip in 1981, bringing more innovation to the already huge

California movement. He was the first-ever owner and chef to create an open kitchen allowing customers to watch their food preparation in front of them. He worked with an enormous grill and a wood-burning oven for his pizzas, two aspects that are present in several restaurants and pizzerias around the world today. He strove to serve affordable food that was healthy, casual, and very fresh (Wine History Project, Agran).

Two years after opening Spago, Puck opened his first fusion restaurant, Chinois. Here, he experimented with Asian style within his casual cuisine. He just wanted to make Chinese food his own way (Wine History Project, Agran).

Puck has made a living off being unpredictable and confident. After working at top-tier restaurants in France, he was bold enough to redefine what high-quality food meant in America by creating simple yet delicious menus that included basic favorites like pizza or orange chicken. He shocked several of his regulars when he opened a Chinese restaurant after the success of Spago, but he did not care. He just wanted to cook what he liked (Wine History Project, Agran).

According to the 2014 *Fast Company* article titled "5 Brilliant Business Lessons from Wolfgang Puck," Puck is not shy of the limelight. He has been a regular on *Good Morning America* since 1986, had an eponymous show on the Food Network, and a weekly food column syndicated in thirty newspapers. He is also active in philanthropy. In 1982, he cofounded the Puck-Lazaroff Charitable Foundation. This foundation, which has raised more than fifteen million so far, supports the annual American Food & Wine Festival, which also supports Meals on Wheels.

He also now has his own company named after him, which has just patented the Wolfgang Puck Pressure Oven. In a 2014 article by *Fast Company* titled "5 Brilliant Business Lessons from Wolfgang Puck," Puck told them, "Lots of chefs put their names on products from other companies. We develop our own appliances and pots and pans. My partners, Sydney Silverman and Mike Sanseverino, and I work on each appliance and go back and forth until it's right. You have to be very careful with your brand...."

His impact on California dining has made his name synonymous with the California Cuisine movement. This is attributed largely to his energy and larger-than-life persona. Now in his sixties, his entrepreneurial spirit and love for cooking have not died. He has truly embraced innovation and artistry. The *Fast Company* article includes a breathtaking photo by Mark Mainz, which previews his brilliantly placed food and decor at The Governors Ballroom on January 6, 2005, in Hollywood, California.

He has a Wolfgang Puck restaurant in Los Angeles, which I have visited on countless occasions with my family when they are in town. The roasted salmon and pesto chicken paillard are our favorite dishes. According to Puck's personal website, he launched the Wolfgang Puck Companies, the umbrella company of Wolfgang Puck Fine Dining Group, Wolfgang Puck Worldwide, Inc., and Wolfgang Puck Catering. The Wolfgang Puck Company handles the operation of twenty fine-dining restaurants (several in the Top Forty Restaurants in the United States), premium catering services, more than eighty Wolfgang Puck Express stores, and kitchen and food merchandise. He is even thinking about expanding his hospitality reach by entering the hotel industry.

***

These three chefs exhibit the success one can have when establishing a fresh, farm-to-table system that utilizes ingredients close to home in an effective way. They truly helped revolutionize and push for a new way of fine dining that has impacted the way chefs worldwide cater to and serve their customers. Looking at the 2022 restaurant landscape today, it is easy to witness how much this movement has impacted and inspired the young chefs of today. The benefit restaurateurs and chefs gain from following a farm-to-table method, like the above chefs did, is tenfold as they create a menu that is authentic to their region while also creating powerful partnerships with local farmers and serving food that is incredibly fresh and tasty.

Ultimately, the Culinary Revolution was born in California, and many believe its inspiration came from the Free Speech movement, which forced many Americans to reevaluate what they eat due to socio-political issues. Many chefs contributed to the overall movement sprouting from the San Francisco Bay Area, but Alice Waters' Chez Panisse is often credited with trailblazing the farm-to-table philosophy that has forever changed the way chefs prepare their food and the way customers experience restaurants today.

No longer are many restaurants relying on processed foods from grocery stores or shipping in ingredients from all over the world. Today, many restaurants thrive off creating concepts that spotlight the local food grown where their restaurant exists. Not only does it help in creating concepts that prioritize fresh ingredients, but it also often pushes for a healthier, more balanced menu. Thanks to the visionary mindsets of chefs like Tower, Waters, and Puck.

CHAPTER 5

THE EVER-CHANGING AMERICAN DIET: PLANTS, PLANTS, AND MORE PLANTS

———

"Vegetarian food leaves a deep impression on our nature. If the whole world adopts vegetarianism, it can change the destiny of humankind."

—ALBERT EINSTEIN

According to the National Health and Nutrition Examination Survey, vegans and vegetarians accounted for just over 2 percent of Americans ten years ago. Some people saw it as a fad or a limited diet that was impossible to maintain. But these diet lifestyles and their motivations have quickly become an important sector of American culture. Well over 5 percent of Americans now identify as vegans or vegetarians, according to a survey and graph included in an Animal Charity Evaluators 2018 article and conducted by Food Surveys, which is a powerful company that assesses food consumption as well as related behavior through insightful surveys.

There are whole companies dedicated to the diet, so veganism is more than a fad in America at this point. There are stores dedicated to the lifestyle, such as The Vegan Warehouse, VegeWholesale, or BESTIES Vegan Paradise. Major healthy grocery store chains, such as Trader Joe's and Whole Foods, have adopted a lot of vegetarian items and even branded themselves in such a way. Emerging from a wave of resistance against the mass production and over-processing of food and other consumable products, what we put into our bodies has become one of our most significant concerns.

Eating healthy is a cultural movement, and veganism is at the forefront of this transformation.

Whether it is due to health, to protect the environment, or to protect animals, veganism has become a mainstream diet in America and all over the world. According to a 2021 Sentient Media article, veganism is predicated on the act of compassion while actively getting rid of all the products from animals in your diet. It is a known fact the majority of animal products in the United States come from factory farms where animals receive poor treatment, enduring conditions many consumers find unacceptable, like confinement, mutilations, and slaughter methods. A vegan diet exclusively allows for plant-based foods such as nuts, vegetables, fruits, and grains. Vegans cannot consume eggs, meat, milk, or even honey.

Veganism is growing exceptionally in countries like the United States, Canada, the UK, and even Australia. According to that same 2021 Sentient Media article, despite the remaining popularity of meat products, retail sales of vegan products continue to rise exponentially, becoming more widely available. The plant protein sector is also growing as more are choosing to invest. Incredibly, there was a 300 percent increase in vegans within the US from 2004 to 2019, equating to more than ten million people converting. Flexitarianism, which I identify as, is also on the rise. It is a term to denote people who eat less meat and are vegetarian a lot of the time. People who label themselves as meat-eaters have decreased from 85 percent in 2019 to 71 percent in 2021.

A 2016 survey within that Sentient article found that the number of people who identify as vegan rose 360 percent in one decade. This global movement could definitely be the result of more global awareness of the connection between meat consumption and heart disease. Sentient shares that Germany has become a vast vegetarian hub, with many vegan restaurants and stores popping up in recent years. About 1.3 million Germans identify as vegan, while eight million identify as vegetarian. Like Germany, Israel created a popular vegan movement and a thriving alternative protein sector as well. India, a country with a history of activism against violence, has a robust population of between 20 to 40 percent of people who identify as vegetarians. Vietnam and Jamaica both have significant vegetarian communities as well.

In America, according to a PBS article titled "From Pythagorean to Pescatarian: The Evolution of Vegetarianism," when William Metcalfe and his wife Susanna arrived in the United States in 1817, they founded an American branch of the Bible Christian Church, the first vegetarian church in the United States. In 1821, he published a pamphlet of a sermon entitled *On Abstinence from the Flesh of Animals*.

Many noteworthy individuals throughout United States history practiced vegetarianism at a young age. Most notably, Benjamin Franklin was inspired by Thomas Tyron's *The Way to Health and Long Life* at sixteen. According to *Time's* 2008 article "A Brief History of Veganism," the first vegetarian society was formed in 1847 in England. Just three years after this, Reverend Sylvester Graham, the inventor of Graham Crackers, cofounded the American Vegetarian Society.

So, what does this mean for the restaurant industry? It implies a need for adaptation by including vegan options on the menu. Companies such as Quorn, Morningstar Farms, Beyond Meat, and Impossible Foods make it possible for popular restaurants to adopt vegan-friendly items. We can see the influence within fast food already, with Quorn's Imposter Burger, the Impossible Whopper at Burger King, the Beyond Burritos at Del Taco, the Impossible Sliders at White Castle, and the charbroiled Beyond Famous Star at Carl's Junior. Vegans now have many options at famous burger joints and even some MLB ballparks, which offer several vegan options.

According to a 2019 *Forbes* article by Brian Kateman, the rise in veganism and vegetarianism in the United States has inspired exclusively vegan restaurants too. A new entrepreneur looking to create a powerful restaurant concept should consider this an option. Today, there is an entire website entitled Happy Cow that acts as a Yelp for vegan and vegetarian restaurants, spotlighting over 24,000 vegetarian-friendly eateries and 1,474 exclusively vegan restaurants.

In 2019, Los Angeles-based vegan chef Matthew Kenney opened his first restaurant in Rhode Island called Plant City. Fittingly named, it's an entirely plant-based, two hundred twenty-five-seat food complex. The complex houses all of

Kenney's vegan creations in one spot: Double Zero (vegan pizza), New Burger (vegan burgers), Bar Verde (vegan Mexican), a coffee bar, a smoothie and juice spot, and even a vegan grocery marketplace with locally grown products. The wildly popular vegan complex has become a very profitable business for Kenney. He explains he was inspired by the food halls in Europe and Eataly's food company, always wanting to do plant-based versions of those (Kateman 2019).

Southern states in the US, known for slow-cooked meaty comfort food, are even entering the vegan food industry. You can find some of the United States' most famous and celebrated vegan and vegetarian institutions south of the Mason-Dixon Line. Most notably, Copper Branch in Ft. Lauderdale, Florida serves an entirely plant-based menu that has a mission of fueling locals with healthy ingredients.

That 2019 *Forbes* article included Founder Rio Infantino's statement, "Copper Branch is a beautiful mission in our efforts to serve gourmet plant-based foods conveniently to the mainstream market. This is real power food! This is food I want my children to eat." Infantino started in the fast-food industry and suffered from considerable weight gain due to a lack of nutritious intake like some other chefs. Because of this consistent unhealthiness and his need to change, he established Copper Branch as a statement to commit to healthy eating for himself and his customers.

Some other popular vegan restaurants in the South include Plant in Asheville, North Carolina, Café Sunflower in Atlanta, and Breads in Oak in New Orleans (Kateman 2019).

The cheese-infested Midwest has also succeeded with vegan restaurants. For example, The Herbivorous Burger is a highly rated vegan burger shop in Minneapolis. Incredibly, the 100 percent vegan patty and cheeseburger joint was started by Aubrey and Kale Walch back in 2014 as a stand at the farmers market. After a successful Kickstarter campaign, the restaurant became a national favorite, drawing the attention of Eater LA, *USA Today*, and Buzzfeed. Café Gratitude, a restaurant chain that started in the San Francisco Bay Area, moved to Kansas City in 2012 and has become a hot spot for locals who enjoy their gourmet plant-based dishes. The Chicago Diner in Chicago has even been serving vegetarian patties and vegan milkshakes since 1983, and Detroit Vegan Soul has multiplied since 2012 from a delivery service to a fully operating vegan restaurant with two popular locations in the city. Like chef Infantino's restaurant in Florida, Vegan Soul's mission is to help make the Detroit population happier while decreasing health-related diseases (Kateman 2019).

According to a 2021 Shondaland article by award-winning author Chelsea Greenwood, some Michelin star chefs are also transitioning to completely meatless menus. Dominique Crenn of San Francisco's Atelier Crenn, Alexis Gauthier of London's Gauthier Soho, and Daniel Humm of New York City's Eleven Madison Park. These chefs are driven by sustainability and thinking about the future of American society. Dana Hunnes, PhD, a community health professor at UCLA, would approve Humm's move, declaring that moving from animal-based foods to plant-based foods reduces carbon emissions and waste byproducts while adding up to 49 percent to the global food supply.

"It is time to redefine luxury as an experience that serves a higher purpose and maintains a genuine connection to the community," Humm explained in a public letter to his loyal customers on his website. "A restaurant experience is about more than what's on the plate. We are thrilled to share the incredible possibilities of plant-based cuisine while deepening our connection to our homes: both our city and our planet." His trendy restaurant now features a $335 multi-course tasting menu which includes fried peppers with Swiss chard, cucumber with melon, and smoked daikon.

Whether inspired by saving animals, the planet, or one's own life, plant-based menus and food options seem to be the clear future of the restaurant industry. Although many Americans are still carnivores, the demand for vegan restaurants and food has never been higher. Therefore, restaurateurs should consider building concepts that promote a new healthy standard because many want and need healthier lifestyles.

At the end of the day, whether a restaurateur decides to go all the way vegan or halfway, to reflect the American diet, restaurants must incorporate plant-based meals and healthy drinks on their menu.

Because different people define fit differently, customization is often critical to pleasing the customer. A few options to please customers could be offering a choice of ingredients or delivering home meal kits with premeasured ingredients. For example, there has been a considerable increase in the popularity of vegan meal kits from Purple Carrot, Mosaic Foods, Fresh n' Lean, HelloFresh, and Daily Harvest. The widening of this market can be attributed directly to people desiring to become healthier in their daily lives and having a convenient delivery option to rely on during their busy lives.

Transparency is also vital because customers want to know what exactly they are consuming. For example, a label with specified calories and key nutritional facts such as fats, carbs, and sugars is essential to helping a customer decide if a particular meal works for them. It may take extra work to figure out specific content information, but it is vital to serving honesty to customers and delicious food. For example, people who follow other health-conscious diets, such as gluten-free, keto, or whole-thirty diets are customers who will want to check nutrition facts.

Today, several successful restaurants exemplify the advantages of switching over to a meatless menu. It is an industry that is not monopolized, so the barrier to entry is fair, though the creativity one can have when curating a menu may be challenging. Still, it offers excellent creative freedom, conceptually.

For example, according to their green and gray website, J. Shelby's in Minnesota is a trendy vegan restaurant similar to many American counter-serve restaurants, but everything served is entirely plant-based. The menu includes seitan-bacon topped salads, cauliflower wings, healthy bowl options, and a vegan spin on the classic Juicy Lucy. Their burgers consist of a house-made Beyond Burger mixture that includes gooey cheese and whole-grain buns. The fact that customers can enjoy a vegan Juicy Lucy that is just as delicious but completely cruelty-free should entice many meat-lovers to visit.

Vedge, in Philadelphia, has the power to convert any meat lover because of its bold flavors. When looking at their beautifully designed website, a hungry customer can see that the incredible married chefs Richard Landau and Kate Jacoby use locally grown vegetables to prepare dishes traditionally served with meat. For example, the restaurant serves portobello carpaccio, featuring caper puree and shaved kale. Their menu also features a wood-roasted carrot kimchi "Rueben" with sauerkraut, carrot mustard, and pumpernickel. The desserts include dairy-free Meyer lemon cheesecake and sticky toffee pudding. They also offer great wine, beer, and creative cocktails to drink with your meal.

"Grab a seat at our agave-based bars" is the motto of Gracias Madre West Hollywood, according to their website. The killer south of the border joint is based in Los Angeles and offers outstanding Mexican food that is wholly meatless and includes all the classics you crave. Enchiladas con mole, traditionally served with chicken, is instead filled with grilled mushrooms, cashew crema, sautéed greens, and black beans. They also have unmatched grain bowls that feature various ingredients like braised lentils, peanut sauce, spinach, coconut rice, pineapple habanero salsa, pumpkin seeds, Pico, and so much more. The owners of Café Gratitude created the Los Angeles destination. The trendy bar is packed with Los Angelenos wanting to try the organic agave smoked cocktails or alcoholic snow cones on weekends.

According to a 2021 *VegNews* article, By CHLOE has changed the perception of vegan restaurants. Located in New York City, By CHLOE featured a menu of creative salads, sandwiches, and vegetarian burgers always in high demand. Their classic burger features a tempeh-lentil-chia-walnut patty with beet ketchup and special sauce. The Guac Burger that they serve has become a massive deal in New York and features a patty that seems like meat but is not. The patty is made from black beans, quinoa, and sweet potato and is topped with corn salsa, onion, guacamole, chipotle aioli, and tortilla chips, all held together in a whole-grain bun. Even though the restaurant had to rebrand as Beatnic following a lengthy legal battle, the menu will remain primarily vegan and celebrate the trailblazing path that By CHLOE created in the vegan market.

Truly's Blog *Beyond Ordinary* spotlights a few vegan food trends that will occur in 2022. One is called the 5:2 Diet, which is a diet that features a meatless eating experience for one month of the year followed by a regular diet for the rest of the year. Vegan chocolate is also growing in popularity, with Cocomels, Hu Nativa, Panda Chocolate, and Raaka leading the way. Vegan eggs are also on the rise and are free of any cholesterol.

Ultimately, as our world becomes more aware of the connection between health problems and consuming animal meat, many more are turning to or at least giving vegetarianism a chance within their lives. The options of vegans and vegetarians alike are extraordinarily diverse and growing from restaurants to food items to delivery services. As a flexitarian who only consumes fish and chicken, I can account that I feel energized and focused in my days, never feeling fatigued or slowed down after I eat. I believe the vegetarian and vegan populations will continue to increase worldwide, with more and more communities building off each other and inspiring more restaurants and grocery stores to rethink their menus and overall concepts.

CHAPTER 6

THE RISE OF WOMEN CHEFS

———

"The more you know, the more you can create. There's no end to imagination in the kitchen."

—JULIA CHILD

Dining in restaurants was deemed "unladylike" during the nineteenth century. Later, segregation between women's and men's dining rooms was established to ensure women were safe from the "dangers" of bold and impolite men. According to Las Vegas' Mob Museum, the Prohibition era allowed for females to begin to dine, get involved in politics, and vote in every single American state. These possibilities were advanced due to the Eighteenth Amendment passing prohibition and the Nineteenth Amendment, which gave the right for all women to vote.

According to an article posted on Prohibition: An Interactive History, the social mobility of women during the nineteenth century greatly influenced the temperance movement and allowed women to be the driving force behind the cause. In aligning the suffrage movement and the prohibition movement, the right to vote was pushed forward and favored by Americans. This hugely impactful era in the history of women's rights gave women the power to speak up for themselves, lending them autonomy to own their businesses and change the world themselves. This development foreshadows the transforming restaurant industry today.

The world wars forced many women to cook, albeit most had to stay home. According to a PSU journal written by Alicia Depler of Franklin & Marshall College, called *American Women in World War Two*, the rationing during World War II specifically caused many women to put extra effort into stocking and preparing home-cooked meals. Rather than visit the grocery store every day, as they could only go so often, women had to get used to using their refrigerators and being creative. This development forced many women to become chefs in their own homes, making the most of whatever food was available.

According to her 2018 biography, posted on Biography.com, Julia Child, one of the most famous female chefs of all time, moved to Washington, DC to boldly volunteer as a research assistant for the Office of Strategic Services. Through this position, Child was sent on missions throughout the world. While working there, Child wed fellow OSS employee Paul Child. Her husband's reassignment to the US Information Service at the American Embassy in Paris pushed Child to explore French cuisine while attending Le Cordon Bleu. Child later opened the cooking school L'Ecole de Trois Gourmandes with classmates, but her success would not have been possible if not for World War II's impact on her decision making as a woman with more autonomy.

However, the emerging cooking culture among women in the domestic sphere rarely extended to professional opportunities.

According to a *Grub Street* article posted by Rachel Sugar, being a chef was a blue-collar job that excluded most women until the Food Network began in 1993. The Food Network displayed women globally, allowing them to share their voices and skills in the kitchen. Two women who were part of the program early on were Donna Hanover and Sara Moulton. The cofounder and former president of the Food Network, Reese Schonfeld, asked Hanover to cohost one of the first shows called *Food News and Views*. These opportunities granted to these women established the Food Network as a big proponent of female chefs. They led to wildly successful female chef television personalities like Giada De Laurentiis, Rachel Ray, and Cat Cora.

Famously, in 2013, there was a *Time Magazine* cover with the title, "The Gods of Food," featuring three men. The article within the magazine was entitled "The 13 Gods of Food," but none of the "Gods" were female. In 2019, only 24 percent of head chefs were female and female chefs made only seventy-six cents to every dollar a male chef made according to the US Bureau of Labor Statistics. 2019's list of the World's 50 Best Restaurants only included nine restaurants owned by females.

Gender equality is still far from the norm in the restaurant industry today. Niki Nakayama, a famous chef, featured on the Netflix food show, *Chef's Table*, explained to the media outlet Shondaland, "The criticisms I sometimes face often make me wonder if a male chef would receive the same scrutiny." Nakayama continues overcoming gender discrimination despite being a well-established, Michelin-starred chef who works in Los Angeles, home to a prime industry of restaurants. Similarly, Janine Booth, a James Beard Award finalist from Australia, admitted to Shondaland, "Even as an owner of restaurants, I have had people, both men and women, doubt my talents and drive and try to bring me down—some behind my back, and some directly to my face." With all these obstacles, it can be difficult for women to secure respect, let alone success.

However, according to Chelsea Greenwood's 2021 Shondaland article, "The Triumph of Women Chefs," there has been a considerable surge of successful restaurants with women head chefs in recent years. There are almost twenty Michelin-star female chefs today. This is incredible, given women were not even allowed in restaurants a century ago. Several legends in today's popular culinary culture are female and include:

- Dolester Miles, who made a name for herself with her homemade desserts; her coconut-pecan cake and lemon meringue tart are favorites at Highlands Bar & Grill, open since 1982 in Birmingham. The James Beard Foundation named her Outstanding Pastry Chef in May 2018.

- Alice Waters, who revolutionized California Cuisine by incorporating farm-to-table and eliminating the brigade-kitchen model at her Michelin-star restaurant, Chez Panisse, in Berkeley, California. She received the Lifetime Achievement Award from the James Beard Foundation in 2004 and the National Humanities Medal in 2014.

- Leah Chase, who was a legendary chef in the South and promoted African American art since the Civil Rights Movement of the 1960s. She also served incredible Creole cuisine, and the James Beard Foundation inducted her into its Who's Who of Food & Beverage in America in 2010.

- Dominique Crenn, who is a French chef that came to San Francisco to found Antelier Crenn, the first female-owned restaurant to earn three Michelin stars in the United States. The gourmet chef also juggles ownership of Bar Crenn and Petit Crenn.

- Gabriele Hamilton, who has become famous for Prune, a popular restaurant that opened in 1999 in the East Village. The trendy spot was included in Anthony Bourdain's PBS show The Mind of a Chef.

- Anito Lo, who became the first woman to cook for a White House state dinner in 2015. She was Iron Chef and was a contestant on Top Chef Masters. Annisa, her New York City restaurant, won a Michelin star and received three stars from the New York Times.

- Nancy Silverton, who single-handedly produced the '90s rise of artisanal bread at La Brea Bakery in Los Angeles. After popularizing sourdough, she cofounded Osteria Mozza, which won a Michelin star in 2008, but she could not stop there as she cofounded Pizzeria Mozza and Mozza2Go.

- Cristeta Comerford, who has served as the first female executive chef of the White House since 2005. She's a Le Club des Chefs member, an exclusive global culinary organization.

- Suzanne Goin, a nine-time James Beard Award nominee for Outstanding Chef and runs a restaurant empire in Los Angeles, including a.o.c., Lucques, Tavern, Larder, one bakery, one marketplace, and Hollywood Bowl Food + Wine.

These talented women have redefined what it means to be a female chef in America: dominant, trailblazing, and unique.

THREE ELITE CHEFS

According to Katherine LaGrave's 2019 *Vogue* article, "Meet the Women Behind Minneapolis's Food Revolution," Minnesota has seen a steady rise in female chefs and owners. Three of the five finalists for the 2018 James Beard Award: Midwest, were from Minneapolis: Ann Kim, Jamie Malone, and Christina Nguyen—three elite chefs. Incredibly, two of the three chefs are immigrants or have come from immigrants.

Minneapolis has become a popular destination for many travelers, not because of the beautiful weather or incredible monuments, but for its bustling and impressive food scene. It has food that reflects the changing demographics, like a population of color increasing faster than anywhere else in the country since 2010. According to LaGrave, Minneapolis was named the fourth-best city globally for young female entrepreneurs and is the second-best city for working women and women who outperform men in profit. These facts make for a restaurant scene that is nothing short of female-dominated.

ANN KIM

The Minneapolis suburb of Apple Valley was not always as it is today. It was sleepy and homogeneous a few decades ago, containing little diversity in culture and culinary options. Ann Kim moved to Apple Valley from South Korea with her parents, grandmother, and sister in 1977 at four. Growing up, if they wanted Korean food, they had to cook it themselves, and they did, fermenting their soybeans for "doenjang" soybean paste and "gojuchang," a spicy chili pepper paste. Although the act brought the family together in their heritage, Kim found it highly embarrassing that they had to make their food at home rather than venturing out to a local Korean restaurant.

Growing up in a white community forced Kim to change who she was to fit in because she did not want to stand out negatively. Eating Korean food made Kim feel different and less than. She did not like being different, but as soon as she realized this food was part of her identity and meant a lot to her parents, she began to take pride in it. However, Kim started to eat it at such a young age and appreciated its uniqueness within the culinary world. It molded her into the champion chef she is today.

Kim's passion for cooking was not inherent. Instead, she went to school at Columbia University in New York City, dreaming of pursuing acting. Ironically, after eight years, Kim left the industry because of its unpredictability and uncontrollable nature, only to enter another unpredictable sector.

In 2007, Kim's then-boyfriend, Conrad Leiffer, inspired her to enter the restaurant industry by encouraging her and offering her advice. Kim had been toying for a long time with the concept of bringing New York-style pizza to the Twin Cities. Her impeccable drive led her to San Francisco, where she did an apprenticeship with Tony Gemignani, a thirteen-time world pizza champion. In 2009, with Leiffer's help, she opened Pizzeria Lola, which would become Hello Pizza two years later.

After the success of the pizza establishment, Kim and Leiffer created their most ambitious and acclaimed restaurant to date: a diverse bar food menu and specialty cocktails. The pair called it Young Juni, after the names of their mothers. Due to the creativity on the menu, with items such as Korean BBQ pizza and chicory Caesar salad, Kim was awarded the 2019 James Beard Award. She says she is still inspired by storytelling because the restaurant industry is like producing a show every day, just with a different stage. Kim's love of the dramatic arts and her family's home cooking has inspired her to become one of the world's greatest chefs. She has blazed a trail for women to flourish in the restaurant industry, especially in Minnesota (LaGrave, *Vogue*).

JAMIE MALONE

Jamie Malone has built a solid culinary presence in Minnesota as well. Her first exposure to food was when she stole a French cookbook while in high school. Reading and following these recipes made her realize she wanted a long career in nutrition. Every weekend, she began to go to the farmers market while listening to *The Splendid Table*. After high school, Malone, being the adventurer she is, would work for a few months to save up money and then spend it on a great vacation worldwide. Eventually, she enrolled in Le Cordon Bleu and received her degree. She started working at the premier spot in Minnesota called La Belle Vie with Tim McKee in 2006, took the head chef position at Sea Change in 2011, and after many accolades, in 2017, moved on to Grand Café in South Minneapolis.

Her ambitious vision for the mainstay restaurant in South Minneapolis garnered international acclaim thanks to dishes like the extravagant savory Paris-Brest made with black honey and chicken liver mousse. The entire restaurant is an audacious depiction of her brain: dishes she loves to create to inspire nostalgic emotions she loves to feel. The inside of the restaurant even houses a 1951 Baker Boy oven and handmade palm-frond wallpaper from Paris. In 2019, Malone told *Vogue* author LaGrave that anyone who enters a kitchen and works hard would be successful because you will be befriended easily and learn quickly. It sounds like many success stories: find a great kitchen and work your butt off until you cannot work anymore, and then some (LaGrave, *Vogue*).

CHRISTINA NGUYEN

Christina Nguyen's food career started with her love of a steaming hot bowl of pho after church in St. Paul. Although Nguyen could experience the delectable treat every Sunday, she could never visit Vietnam, the country both her parents fled in the 1970s. Her parents met at the University of Minnesota, got married, and had Christina. Her parents had always thought she would never leave Minnesota, but Nguyen wanted to experience the country where her parents had emigrated from. So, she went, without hesitation and on her own, after college. Surprisingly, despite experiencing some culture shock, Nguyen felt like she belonged there. However, her first restaurant endeavor upon her return had nothing to do with Vietnam but instead was called Hola Arepa, a South American sandwich joint.

Her Vietnamese roots later shone through in her 2017 restaurant, Hai Hai, a funny play on words for the strip club it replaced called Double Deuce. However, what made Nguyen's award-winning establishment stand out was not original Vietnamese flavors such as the pho she enjoyed on Sundays, but the outrageous flavors she developed, like water fern cakes and banana blossom salads. She was also inspired by other countries such as Indonesia and the Philippines when coming up with the dishes. Her standout success led to her selection as a semifinalist at the James Beard Awards. Nguyen, who is usually never emotional, was moved to tears when she realized she, Malone, and Kim, were nominated for Best Chef: Midwest, three persistent women chefs from Minneapolis.

Three very different women being nominated for the top prize in the Midwest is enormous in the food industry, which has been historically male-dominated. These three chefs exemplify what hard work can achieve on every level. Their passion and genuine attention to detail have enabled their enduring success in the face of doubt or any misogynistic naysayers.

The fact that these strong women were able to curate brands for themselves in a world that has become so male-dominated for much of this century displays the ability for females to pave a strong path for their futures in the restaurant industry. The future of women chefs within the industry is seemingly brighter than ever, and as avid customers of the industry, we will continue to see them grow and flourish to new levels that no person has achieved before.

Racheal Ray, Giada De Laurentiis, Nigella Lawson, Cat Cora, and other big female names in the industry who have sold books, created shows, and opened restaurants illustrate that there is no ideal profile or personality type for a successful business owner within the industry. The rise of female chefs illustrates that a fine-dining restaurant can be led and owned by any gender, and further, any race, ethnicity, or political standing.

If you have star power, nothing will get in your way. Let it shine. The only obstacle stopping one from being successful is their own predetermined way of thinking. As humans, it is our job to unlearn stereotypes and rewrite what we believe to be the status quo. Restaurateurs and chefs can help write that next page for the restaurant industry chapter (LaGrave, *Vogue*).

PART 2

LET'S EAT: MAJOR KEYS TO SUCCESS

CHAPTER 7

TASTY FOOD STARTS WITH A SOURCE AND A CHEF

———

"Food brings people together on many different levels. It's the nourishment of the soul and body. It's truly love."

—GIADA DE LAURENTIIS

Imagine leaving America and being so in love with the food that you create a restaurant because you love processed, greasy, and sweet treats so much. I picture a menu combination of cornbread, fried chicken, mac and cheese, grits, tater tots, salmon, key lime pie, or a banana split for dessert.

When discovering the best restaurants in the United States, that is often the story: foreigners bringing their tastes from home to surprise Americans with their authentic flavors and family setting. For California restaurants Centonove and Anatolian, that story sounds familiar. When I spoke with them directly, the owners claimed their connection to their food allows them to serve customers with happiness and care and offer home-cooked meals made with love and fresh ingredients.

Centonove is an Italian restaurant located at 109 W. Main Street in downtown Los Gatos, my hometown. Centonove means 109 in Italian. The restaurant is owned by ChargePoint CEO Pasquale Romano and his wife Andrea Romano, who runs the day-to-day operations. Mr. Romano was an investor in the business and desired to create a successful and traditional Italian restaurant with a modern twist. His parents are both fantastic cooks, who make Italian cuisine fresh, and he learned to cook by helping them.

Mrs. Romano says she learned to cook a lot through her husband and some from her Italian grandmother, who would have the whole family over on Sunday nights, where Mrs. Romano says she always ate more than she helped make. "We both love Italy and the Italian culture," she said. "We are both dual citizens, and we plan on purchasing a second home on the Amalfi coast shortly. Both of Pasquale's parents are amazing cooks." The Romanos did not try to be complex in terms of menu design. They instead decided on Italian cuisine and incorporated their favorite dishes.

The couple is proud of their strong Italian roots. Mr. Romano's father was born in Italy and immigrated to the US when he was nineteen and grew up in an Italian-speaking household, learning to cook from his father and mother. He wanted a restaurant that reflected authentic Italian cuisine. To coincide with this genuine pursuit of a family style restaurant inspired by his mom and pops, the Romanos avoided mass marketing and huge portions, the kind of restaurants that many Americans visit.

To create robust and accurate Italian flavor, the Romanos employ Italian chefs, and the chef they opened Centonove with was Italian. After leaving, they had to have a Sous Chef step up and keep the original chef's menu. Sadly, that chef tragically passed from COVID-19 in February of 2021. Wanting to get back to having a head chef who was very familiar with Italian cuisine, they desired to hire a true Italian who understood both the culture and flavor profiles they desired.

Centonove has one executive chef, originally from Napoli, who has been in the States for six years. They also have many line cooks, prep cooks, and one Sous Chef. Davide, a chef from Napoli, received complete autonomy over the menu by the Romanos with only a few restrictions. He dreams up specials regularly while also changing the ingredients and dishes to reflect what is seasonally available. The Romanos understood a quality restaurant starts with a chef who has genuinely invested in the craft and values the actual concept of the restaurant. Rather than rely on great marketing, the genuineness of their mission to acquire a talented chef made all the difference.

***

Like catching a star chef, an owner must also develop star ingredients.

"When I go to the market, I know what to buy." These were the simple yet precise words of Dino Tekdemir, owner of a Turkish restaurant, Anatolian, in Palo Alto, California as we sat down to talk. Tekdemir also owns Naschmarkt in Campbell, California and Nemea Greek Taverna in San Jose, California. He claims the restaurant's success rides on his use of quality, homegrown ingredients. He takes home the same ingredients he desires to be cooked in his restaurant. To make Anatolian feel at home, he creates a menu replicating much of what he ate when he was growing up in Turkey as a young kid.

Tekdemir grew up in a household with fifteen siblings. They had sheep and grew up with a lot of cheese and yogurt in every meal. His father was also involved in the agriculture industry. The farm-to-table transformation caught Tekdemir's attention and began his interest in the food industry. For Tekdemir, opening Anatolian to bring Turkish food to Silicon Valley was all about reliving memories through the food. As we sat outside his beautiful restaurant decorated with furniture and art from Turkey, he called over his waiter to give us his favorite Turkish black tea. He smiled ear to ear. "This is important to me. I love it. It's important to make someone comfortable only through maximizing my childhood memories because it brings you back."

The chef and owner retired from his daily work in the restaurant in March 2020, and wow, he can take care of his daughter while keeping a birds-eye view of his three restaurants from his house in Palo Alto next to the Stanford University campus. He has vacationed to Hawaii, Malibu, and Turkey since he has been off, understanding and appreciating the plethora of ingredients each place offers. While in Maui, he met with famous farm-to-table chef Roy Yamaguchi to discuss creating an ultimate restaurant: home-style cooking. For Tekdemir, he models his food after what his family likes. He declares that the food he serves is always his number one priority.

This mentality means he always eats and drinks while thinking critically about it and its relationship with his customers, whom he considers his "family."

Tekdemir knows Anatolian presents an engaging dining experience because Mediterranean food is delicious and healthy. California has become a very vegan-friendly state, and Anatolian provides a vast array of fresh and hearty vegetarian options to choose from. Tekdemir kindly served me one of his most popular appetizer dishes: the Combo Appetizer that comes with hummus, tabouleh, baba ghanoush, cacik, dolma, falafel, olives, and piyas. He created dishes from the finest seasonal produce bought at the farmers market or local food source companies and has taken a lot of inspiration from the cuisines of the Mediterranean, curating an exquisite menu featuring dishes meant for sharing. These large plates are all pieces of Tekdemir's vision of an atmosphere of comfortability and family.

It is meaningful to him to strictly use the highest quality, halal-certified food. This standard includes whole animals and fresh fish butchered and prepared daily alongside a selection of locally grown vegetables, sautéed meats, healthy grains, legumes such as chickpeas and beans, and yogurt and olive oil. Unfortunately for Dino, his restaurant inspired by his hometown will shut down at the end of this year after serving Palo Alto proudly for over ten years. Tekdemir is instead growing a chain of his other European restaurant called Naschmarkt. It will be a bittersweet end to a very successful and lucrative run for the restaurant owner, father, and husband. His new endeavor will undoubtedly remain on fresh ingredients and their power to bring his customers together for an unforgettable and nostalgic dining experience.

When opening a restaurant, as exemplified by my discussions with some of my favorite owners in California, it is critical to establish a source and a chef that embody what one desires in their restaurant concept. This fundamental need means that traveling to the country where your food is from may be an essential step in finding a chef that exceeds concept expectations and delivers extraordinarily authentic food.

Envisioning a menu come to life can only be achieved first by developing a strategic plan of discovering the best ingredients like at a local farmers market and creating solid relationships with cooks who inherently bleed your brand theme and concept. The Romanos and Tekdemir expressed how much they value their close relationships with their chefs. This solid foundation is built upon the fact that there is a genuine connection that cannot be broken between the owners and their respective chefs; the intentions are pure and corresponding on every level.

As an owner of any start-up, it is critical to hire people who run an essential part of your business that reflects who you are to represent the brand you envision fully. When two similar people come together with one mission and goal in mind, the possibilities multiply, and the potential for success is a lot higher.

CHAPTER 8

PROMOTE POSITIVITY

___

HOW TO NURTURE AND CREATE AN ENVIRONMENT THAT SOLIDIFIES CUSTOMER RELATIONSHIPS

"Prior planning prevents piss poor
performance."

—GREG KNAPP

"The more you surround yourself with people that are better than you, the better you become." These are the words of Gabriel Stulman in his 2015 interview with *GQ*. Gabriel Stulman is the founder and CEO of Happy Cooking Hospitality, a restaurant group that owns West Village food spots, Joseph Leonard, Jeffrey's Grocery, Fedora, Fairfax, and Bar Sardine. They also own other New York joints like Studio, George Washington Bar, Simon and the Whale, and The Jones.

Stulman developed his love for hospitality at the University of Wisconsin-Madison and worked at a local restaurant. But it all started at an earlier age, when he got to enjoy the Jewish cooking of his mother. He worked as a line cook in high school, making Philly cheesesteaks for Steak n' Things. Stulman opened his restaurant because he needed the tuition to pay UW Madison. He graduated from the University of Wisconsin in 2003 and went straight to New York, his favorite city in the country. Stulman opened his restaurant in the West Village with his wife, Gina, called Joseph Leonard. The restaurant eventually developed into the staple restaurant group, with many deeming him the mayor of West Village. What has revolutionized the way Stulman does business is his study of the art of hospitality and how to drive the best hospitality in the country, beginning with his employees (GQ).

Positive engagement matters so much for any business to succeed, especially in the restaurant industry, where new clients are served daily. A *Harvard Business Review* article titled, "Proof That Positive Work Cultures Are More Productive," explains that high pressure environments lead to stressful workplaces that can induce heart disease, disengagement that can lead to more errors and absenteeism, and lack of loyalty. In the same article, the American Psychological Association estimated that $500 billion is lost from the US economy because of stress while 550 workdays are lost each year due to stress.

Conversely, a positive environment of connection, empathy, and encouragement inspires wellness in employees. In *Give and Take*, Wharton professor Adam Grant describes that kindness and generosity, specifically from leaders, are strong predictors of team and organizational effectiveness. This phenomenon means that a positive leader can inspire chefs to more efficiently deliver their optimal performance and waiters to give excellent service for customers to consider coming back.

According to a 2017 *Forbes* article by Adam Ozimek, 17 percent of restaurants fail in the first year. At the same time, in his engaging 2014 TEDx Talk, "A Winning Recipe—Lessons from Restaurants on Engaging Your Team," Stulman reported from a survey of twenty-five million people that three out of ten people are engaged in their job, five out of ten are disengaged at work, and the last two are actively disengaged. The influx of negative energy and lack of presence is plaguing restaurants.

When was the last time you had a genuine conversation with restaurant staff who cared about your needs and who listened to your ideas without rushing to the following table? Unfortunately, it is often rare in today's world as people feel it is okay to bring their default selves to the workplace. This lack of energy, focus, and enthusiasm can all be turned around with celebration and positive reinforcement.

As a restaurant owner, start by celebrating the individuals working for you; try to gauge their interests authentically. Fully operational restaurant staff should feel like a big family supporting each other. Workers should be saying, "It never feels like work." Engagement should not even be questioned or thought of at any time. To ignite passion, excitement, energy, and pride into guests and colleagues, all you have to do is take an interest in the employees' dreams and ambitions. When people feel cared about and understood, they're more motivated to work their hardest to help you, too. The four steps Emma Seppälä and Kim Cameron discuss in their 2015 *Harvard Business Review* article include: foster social connections, show empathy, go out of your way to help, and encourage people to talk to you—especially about their problems.

On day one, as a manager, you need to be talking to employees to figure out their dreams and ambitions to help them achieve. But, of course, this can be done in small steps; ask fundamental questions and be curious. Allocate time to get to know your staff to talk to them as human beings, so you can gauge their energy, skills, and how they best interact with customers.

As a restaurateur, you must promote teamwork and collaboration. This goal can be achieved through an inclusive attitude and meetings and valuing the opinion of your employees—schedule meetings where different employees within your company will be interested and involved. For example, create three voluntary sessions with bartenders from three restaurants when changing the cocktail list. As a group, allow the team to run through brainstorming, editing, and implementation. This specificity and autonomy allow the entire bar staff to be fully engaged in discussion. Every cocktail added to the list should fuel the employee who chose that cocktail. After, as an owner, support each bartender by enabling them to produce their drink however they make it themselves.

This robust support allows the bartender to take immense pride in their work.

Another actionable item to instill strong teamwork in your business is internal promotion. Internal promotion shares the spotlight with your colleagues and provides positive reinforcement for all the hard work they have already contributed to the company. Many managers promise "career development" and "clear paths for growth." However, these are dull, hollow words that do not fit an authentic restaurant atmosphere that inspires employees to shine in front of loyal customers. The alternative to this is actual connection and a feeling of true purpose when one gets to work each day to better the restaurant.

Gabriel Stulman, who went from making cheesesteak to running six New York City restaurants, told *GQ* in an article written by Justin Fenner in 2015, "I'm a firm believer that the more you surround yourself with people that are better than you, the better you become—if you are competitive." Stulman credits surrounding himself with people that are better than him to become better himself, and this firm affirmation in the people around him, acknowledging their presence and ability, strengthens their ability to deliver. When you believe you are truly surrounded by greatness, you elevate and become greater. Elevating others, therefore, will eventually elevate you as the whole group including yourself will excel to another level through pushing each other.

As an owner, try to amplify stories of promotion. For example, post about or talk about why you choose specific people.

A creative solution to worrying about lack of focus or unfulfilling roles is to promote a general manager of another restaurant to enable him to perform this managerial duty at two of your restaurants. But, of course, this solution only works if you own multiple spots. Still, it rewards the general manager and pushes him to utilize his developed talents at both restaurants, eventually training the following managers.

Another example of a helpful promotion can be promoting two assistant service managers to be service managers while offering bartenders or waiters the new service manager positions. Then, an owner can hire a new bartender or waiter from the outside. That way, internal people are promoted while external people are solely brought in to fill their last position.

Every new person is being trained by the person who just held their position. Therefore, it is essential to promote a less qualified internal candidate over a more qualified external candidate to maintain this cycle. The positive reinforcement will allow employees to feel valued, hopefully, providing a better training experience for the new external employees.

These promotion tactics allow for better training, enrich the company culture, and promote positive retention.

Ultimately, lack of engagement from some employees undermines the ambitions of other employees. Enthusiasm or lack thereof is exceptionally contagious. It only takes one bad apple sometimes to make the whole batch sour. To keep your pack sweet, make a change by celebrating individuality. Promote positive company culture by living out the company's passions inside and outside. Lead by example by creating collaboration, sharing recognition, and promoting internally.

CHAPTER 9

SERVICE MATTERS

———

"Service to others is the rent you pay for
your room here on earth."

—MUHAMMAD ALI

Quality service breeds customer loyalty.

To have a successful start-up business in today's world
requires one aspect more than any other: empathy. Empathy
for the customers who come to you because they are looking
for a quality product and willing to try what you are selling
to fulfill their needs. For an owner to keep that curious customer's attention piqued, there needs to be constant effort to
provide maximum satisfaction.

Entrepreneur, and my mentor, Steve Blank, who I met during
the summer of 2020, has one big lesson for his students: "Get
out of the building to be successful!" Steve has told me this
on multiple occasions when I have pitched ideas to him; an
owner can never find product-market fit unless he or she
actively puts the product in front of wide eyes and opinions.

I left many meetings at Stanford with Steve where my cofounder would feel frazzled because customer development is a continuous process in any successful start-up and often requires continuous pressure. When Steve recites this to his students, he means that for any start-up to have a chance, they need to continuously test their solutions or ideas with the exact people paying for that solution. Many start-ups fail because they fail to listen to their audience. Establish a market surrounding your product and then get to know them inside and out. Put yourselves in the shoes of your customers because the customer is the most essential part of your business.

Without customer turnover, a company is nonexistent.

In a restaurateur world, listening to the customer should be easy. Every day, a restaurant provides a service to people who sit down to enjoy a meal or order some food to go. Venturing outside the building only needs to happen before you open to understand if the population you desire to feed would embrace your unique idea. To know where your hungry customer is coming from, ask genuine questions:

- Did you enjoy the food?
- How was your evening with us?
- What would you order next time?

If the customer is a regular, try to understand what keeps them coming back:

- What's your favorite thing about my restaurant?
- What's your favorite item on the menu?

Sometimes, a customer enjoys the service on a level that is hard to explain, or maybe too simple to put into words. That's where observing your customers daily within your four walls is crucial to analyzing customer satisfaction and loyalty.

According to an article posted on the innovative foodie website Spoon Mob, Aaron Silverman is a famous American chef and restaurateur from Maryland and was awarded the James Beard Foundation Award in 2016. Silverman went to L'Academie de Cuisine to study as a chef and began working under chef Jonathon Krinn. He then worked at a string of restaurants with established chefs, from David Chang's Momofuku to Marco Canora's Insieme to George Mendes' Aldea to Sean Brock's McCrady's Restaurant.

Silverman was determined to open his own unique restaurant after gaining quality experience with America's top chefs. He read David Meyer's *Setting the Table: The Transforming Power of Hospitality in Business* and opened his first restaurant: Rose's Luxury. An electric, New American, homey café and bar in the heart of Washington, DC, Rose's Luxury has been widely considered one of the most successful restaurants in the country.

In his TEDx Talk in 2015, "How I Built the Number One Restaurant in America," Silverman has one word to describe how his food business operation, set in a converted townhouse, became a sensation: service. Silverman credits all the success of his business to the dedication of his employees, who are caring, passionate, and well-dressed. Silverman recommends developing excellent hiring practices, and to do this, Silverman points out that restaurant owners must know what they are looking for and what they are not looking for.

In other words, as a hiring manager, you should be looking for people, not positions. Don't look for people with the necessary skills, but with a strong desire to work with the existing idea and team. Hire people because they want to do the job, not because they can. Don't look at resumes but look at references. Look for great personalities and attitudes.

Silverman now has a second-in-line manager who started as an unpaid intern a year prior with no prior restaurant experience. However, with enthusiasm and understanding, the way she served clients warranted a promotion over any other experienced employee.

"We are not in the restaurant business. We are in the people business," Silverman said. Silverman worked tirelessly to open his first restaurant and made only seven hundred and fifty dollars the first month. He quickly understood he was in the hospitality business not to provide good food or good service but to leave guests feeling excellent and satisfied. This fact meant the food and service were just tools to achieve optimal service. Silverman boldly put the workers before customers and investors because when incredible people want to work for you, and turnover is no longer an issue, everything else falls into place.

Food only accounts for 40 percent of what they do, so success is dependent on workers at the end of the day. So, what makes a business successful in Silverman's eyes? The quality of the product, or the service his chef, bartender, hosts, and servers provide.

My hometown of Los Gatos, a small town in the San Francisco Bay Area at the southwest corner of San Jose in the foothills of the Santa Cruz Mountains, is home to many flourishing restaurants. The Wine Cellar, nestled at the base of the mountains in historic Old Town, has been a Los Gatos favorite since 1966. Hungry customers can dine alfresco on their award-winning patio while enjoying gorgeous views of the Santa Cruz Mountains. They can also explore the renovated basement for an intimate experience, featuring golden-washed walls and candle-lit booths.

I sat down with the current owner of over twenty years, Julie Van Atta, in one of the serene and gold-decorated meeting rooms downstairs. We talked for a gripping two hours, making me late for my friend Greg Knapp's going away dinner in Danville.

When Van Atta started working at the Wine Cellar as a bartender back in the '90s, the historic Los Gatos Old Town was losing money, and many of the restaurants and stores were going bankrupt. There was a lot of hesitancy and doubt when beginning the business, but Van Atta stuck through it, and she owes it all to her team, who worked with her and supported her vision. Van Atta was hopeful when Federal Realty, a significant real estate investment trust, came in and purchased the lot because they only bought places they believed could succeed. When they made the purchase, the Wine Cellar was "a complete disaster and dilapidated with deferred maintenance." This purchase was a significant deal because owners usually only bought places they knew could succeed right off the bat.

Where I was sitting with Van Atta during our interview, a private dining area for special guests, was all dirt at that time. They had to redo everything, starting with the bathrooms. In Van Atta's words: "You get some money, borrow some money and kind of try to see what you can do." At the center of it all, remained her loyal customers.

Van Atta declares earnestly, "For us, as far as what we do here is always customer-driven because it doesn't matter what I like if the customers don't like it." The owner recognizes that this is where many failed restaurateurs go wrong. They don't know their customers, and they continue to evolve without taking their customers into account. The Wine Cellar prides itself on listening to its customers, whether face-to-face feedback on the patio or a Yelp review explaining that the ribs may have been too dry. The attention to detail and prompt responses to customer requests are what Van Atta prioritizes in her wildly successful restaurant.

Of course, every ounce of feedback should be taken with a grain of salt. One customer's opinion should never sway a decision that impacts the whole business, like a menu choice or a specific renovation. However, it is always good to gauge common consensus and act on it to keep customers pleased. Finally, after listening to customer feedback, Van Atta makes decisions that work and can be effective, like holding back salt on some plates, such as the ribs or lasagna.

A common theme arose in my conversation with Van Atta: consistency. She prides herself on making sure her staff feels challenged and loved. Because the Wine Cellar hosts many high net worth regulars or influential individuals who demand a high-quality experience, Van Atta keeps her employees for a while to develop relationships with the customers. From the chefs to the hosts to the servers, several of them stay around for a very long time before leaving because of their connections with customers who are happy to keep coming back. Van Atta says that people rarely quit serving jobs at her restaurant.

This high employee involvement is a testament to the Wine Cellar's winning atmosphere: warm, polished, and welcoming.

Van Atta was quick to reference her employees —eccentric, bold, and brash, right off the bat. She makes it a point to hire people who know how to carry themselves confidently in front of anyone who enters, while being entertaining and flexible. It is a tricky balance, but Van Atta enjoys hiring "characters" and knows how important the staff is to its overall success. The team is filled with eccentric people who love to show off who they are.

This team culture creates a competitive dynamic between the staff that allows them to have fun while supporting each other. Van Atta allows her employees to feel independent and have autonomy. While some restaurants have extended training programs, Van Atta has her new hires shadow for three days before they are thrown directly into the field to show off their talents. Because she trusts her staff, they feel comfortable being themselves and rarely fail to deliver.

Besides managing the restaurant, Van Atta also handles the wine list. She laughs as she says, "I think the biggest thing for us to acknowledge is that there's not a lot of ego involved in decision making. I get the wine list...I don't really care about fancy names. I don't care about obscure names even though we are called the Wine Cellar. I only care about what people want and what seems like a reasonable investment on a list that someone is going to order."

Starting a restaurant alone is very hard. Having a group of cofounders who push each other and support each other unconditionally will build a solid foundation for the future and a team that can maintain reliable service without jeopardizing customer satisfaction. For the Wine Cellar, it has been a family effort. Van Atta's daughters have all worked as hostesses, taking customers to their table. Her dad has helped with the bills by handling the accounting, so she has more time to welcome important clients downstairs. Her husband has also been able to make appearances to welcome guests in.

Over the years, it has become known for its excellent service and the familial bond among the staff, whether by blood or choice.

Returning to Gabriel Stulman from Promoting Positivity, this philosophical restaurateur can teach us about an employee phenomenon that Van Atta has avoided. Stulman developed a passion for the hospitality industry and has worked in many famous NYC restaurants. In his TED Talk, he explained a severe problem: employee engagement. Restaurants have served as a great case study for his assertion because employees must be engaged at all times for the restaurant to succeed.

Restaurants, in general, generate about a 6 percent profit margin. As well, workers must work long hours in a hot environment. There is always high pressure to please customers, deal with a perishable product, the product's life cycle occurs over one day (receive, prep, and serve within a day), and most people are trying to dine at the same hour every night. Stulman hits the nail on the head with his studies, synthesizing one clear message about the restaurant industry that every owner needs to understand: service matters.

Once you know that, as Julie Van Atta and Aaron Silverman learned in their top-notch establishments, you can take more concrete steps in your business, leading to purposefully choosing to promote quality service.

CHAPTER 10

LOCATION CHANGES THE GAME: SPACE AND SAFETY

"A well-run restaurant is like a winning baseball team. It makes the most of every crew member's talent and takes advantage of every split-second opportunity to speed up service."

—DAVID OGILVY

Location is a tricky aspect to master in the restaurant industry. This difficulty is due to owners balancing pay of incredibly high prices and the importance of accessibility to customers through a good enough location. A restaurant's location can drastically change the amount of business it can accumulate. The critical need for a prime location has caused many owners to move to big cities or create close bonds with their landlords, hoping to receive incredible deals.

When deciding on a location, an owner must determine one that is easily accessible to their target demographic. There are many options that one should consider while weighing the potential reward. A kiosk in a mall? A truck that can drive to populated locations? A large space on the corner in a metropolitan city? It all depends on one's value proposition and the population one desires to reach.

Centonove, an Italian restaurant quickly becoming a local favorite in Los Gatos, is filled every weekday and on the weekends. Centonove does serve incredible fresh pasta and flatbread dishes, but a huge aspect of their success has been their location in the center of downtown Los Gatos. The classy spot is located at 109 W Main Street. Owners Andrea and Pasquale Romano have never considered moving because of the prime location, easily accessible to locals walking along Main Street. Los Gatos is a costly town located in South Silicon Valley, bordering the Santa Cruz mountains and San Jose. The couple has been blessed with a considerate landlord who works with them instead of against them.

Via a first-person interview with me, Andrea, general manager of Centonove and nearby restaurant Cin-Cin, described the landlords as excellent allies in the course of their growth in their restaurant business. The generosity and genuine care of landlords can transform the outlook of your business. For the Romanos, the empathy and involvement of their landlord has been paramount to them remaining open and flourishing in their location. He has allowed them to take their time paying bills because of his understanding during the pandemic and his authentic connection with the Romanos.

Andrea exclaimed about her landlord, "She is so engaged in our success and was above and beyond during the shutdowns. Having a wonderful landlord is key. That's not always the case, which is a bummer." Network and try to develop a relationship with a caring landowner. You may be one step closer to a prime property opportunity that could shape the lucrative future for your business.

There are several aspects of the location to keep in mind before making a final decision: parking, visibility, size, space, and the neighboring area.

First, parking must be easily accessible around your restaurant. Otherwise, several people may pass on your product due to laziness or the lack of time or patience to walk. This impatience can be avoided by prioritizing a parking lot next to your restaurant or ensuring you are not located on a busy intersection with a lack of multiple turn-in lanes.

Visibility is also critical, so potential customers who drive by can easily see your sign and what you stand for. I cannot tell you how many times I have been driving on the freeway, and suddenly, I see a sign that advertises incredible-looking food on a building right off the highway. That one sign changed the course of my entire trip because I ended up eating a full course meal with some buddies there and taking a rest stop. Having a large, attractive sign that people can see will allow these spontaneous visits to occur continuously.

The size of your restaurant is somewhat important because there needs to be room for an adequate kitchen, a large walk-in refrigerator depending on your inventory, dry storage, and even office space. On top of all that, there needs to be space for a spacious dining room, a wait station, and potentially, a bar. Considering all these components of a successful business, an owner must have some spatial awareness because the space you are renting will fill up fast.

Some spaces are not made for successful eateries. The unspeakable curse of some locations is that they will never be successful no matter what one puts in them; it's proof of how important a location is to a business. For example, in Los Gatos, a shopping center on the border of San Jose has a Walgreens and has had trouble keeping businesses operating. An Italian restaurant called Gallo's, one of my family's all-time favorite family style places, transformed into a Starbucks that ended up closing. The pandemic added to Starbucks' economic blow, but anytime a Starbucks goes out of business, there must be a problem with the location.

This location was terrible because of the area surrounding it. In past years, there have been shootings around that area, which caused many to avoid it altogether. Places with poor reputations make it difficult for even established restaurant brands to succeed because developing a loyal customer base is an ongoing challenge.

The location also goes hand in hand with safety. When deciding on your site, a restaurateur must know if the building has all the necessary bells and whistles. These essentials include robust wiring, automatic or light doors, fire alarms, sprinkler systems, and proper piping for clean water needed for restrooms.

Neighbors in the area should be considered immediately without question. Like-minded individuals stick together and allow each other to grow. The same is true for restaurants. Successful small businesses located next to each other empower each other, and several people will become customers of all restaurants nearby each other. It is important to remember that your business is different from restaurants nearby because being a direct competitor of a company in the same shopping center may not go over well. So not only will the competitor not enjoy your presence, but you would be competing for customers rather than sharing them.

Last, it is essential to think through your location rather than acting too quickly. Choosing a remote restaurant may be worth it, but it also may be a huge gamble. For example, you may love a restaurant right off the bat, but after sketching out the floor plan, realize it cannot be the one for your ideal vision. You also must see the prospective places you are considering at different times of the week and day.

For example, a property may look like a prime location at noon on the weekdays but then be extremely slow on the weekends. Therefore, it is vital to gauge the excellent business opportunity before matching it to your restaurant style because signing a lease is a big commitment. As a new restaurant owner, try to negotiate a great deal with your landlord that calls for a lease of one to two years rather than five to ten years.

I had the pleasure of speaking with David Perlick, renowned chef and owner of Region in Barrington, Illinois who decided his location out of convenience. Perlick was born and raised in western New York and moved to Crystal Lake, Illinois, in McHenry County at a young age. In 1990, when he was thirteen years old, he began living and working at Italian Gourmet in Algonquin, Illinois. He now lives in Barrington, where he has lived for the last eight years. Perlick decided to stay in Barrington and open his own restaurant business there.

Perlick opened Region, a diverse eatery in Barrington because he lived in the town. With his experience in hospitality,

Perlick had an excellent opportunity to live and work in the same city because he could quickly develop fruitful relationships through business, philanthropy, and the schooling of his children. It was an obvious no-brainer for him to open a business in the town where he lived, especially having commuted a half-hour plus for the last fifteen years.

Perlick is the chef and the owner, so he has developed confidence in both business and cooking. He knows he is good at what he does. "I feel right at home because I am pretty much awesome at a lot that I do. I do have some failures, and without sounding cocky, I have been cooking now for over twenty-five years." He understands the routine and how to execute it, and this experience allowed him to scope out the best kitchen for him to set up shop. He specializes in regional American cooking, and Chicago is a metropolitan mixing pot of food lovers.

When he opened his restaurant, he called it Region because he used many different ingredients and cooking styles inspired by other nationalities. Perlick loves doing what the owner does because it matches up with the makeup of the United States, influenced by the culture's diverse ingredients and styles. He loves the country's diversity, and any Chicagoan or outsider can appreciate that on his menu.

Perlick has quickly established Region as the town's most renowned restaurant because it represents Barrington, former home to indigenous people, stands for cultural appreciation, diversity, and heartiness. Perlick is quick to state that his restaurant is rated 4.9 out of five on public, customer-voted sites like Yelp, meaning how he organizes and manages his business is excellent.

Location and deciding on a site also mean knowing what that population desires. Perlick cooks with a delicate balance of spiciness, saltiness, and textures to adhere to his location's population in Chicago. He enjoys being creative and putting different flavor combinations together, never sticking to his customers' taste buds. He recognizes he is a professional and his Chicagoan customers come to enjoy his unique product because the population has a very high taste and diverse palette, being the metropolitan city that it is.

It can be a slippery slope if an executive chef ever adheres to customers' taste buds. Being unique while representing your location is so important. Knowing how flavors work allows a chef to develop a theme and adhere to its principles. These principles for Perlick were well established before he opened his restaurant, and these principles allowed him to choose his prime location in Barrington.

Choosing the best location possible to create a restaurant that thrives is paramount to succeeding as a restaurant owner. Several restaurants in a shopping center called Walgreens Square close to where I live on the border between Los Gatos and San Jose, have recycled many eateries because the location is removed from the busiest street in my area called Union and there has been some history of violence in that area. What was once one of our favorite Italian restaurants called Gallo's turned into Starbucks, which is now vacant. When choosing where to lease, researching the history of the area is important as well as keeping in mind the price per square footage, the marketing potential, and the ability for customers to easily park and access the restaurant. A fine location leads to a fine-dining experience.

PART 3

THE FUTURE: SHOOT FOR THE MILKY WAY

CHAPTER 11

EMBRACE ADVERSITY

"Cooking is like snow skiing. If you don't fall at least ten times, then you're not skiing hard enough."

—GUY FIERI

Tantalizing salmon over a bed of white rice, sweet and sour pork that tastes spicy when you bite into it but becomes tender and juicy as you chew, and a homey ambiance fit for any average joe to come in and enjoy service, Sushi Lover is owned by an immigrant family from South Korea, who first opened the place as a way of acquiring work visas to stay in California.

Being a restaurateur means being a self-starter and being independent. It is synonymous with being an entertainer. You have to perform to market your idea to ensure other people will also like it as much as you do. This remarkable push is never easy and requires incredibly hard work and determination to keep going even in the face of doubt. Adversity is inevitable in the pursuit of success.

On February 11, 2022, I was chatting with the front man of Young the Giant, a famous rock band that formed in Irvine, California in 2004. Sameer Gadhia was on a Pre-Med track at Stanford University, one of the most prestigious schools in the world, located close to my hometown in Palo Alto, California. However, after much soul-searching and falling down, he realized that the creative world was the best path for him. He left Stanford to pursue music his sophomore year. He exclaimed to me in the business school courtyard of USC, "The happiest points in your life are during your low points between successes." He also advised me to, "Find what you love and then move forward. You can do anything if you have the passion to move forward."

Zazie Beetz, a German American actress known for her role as Vanessa "Van" Keefer in the hit comedy-drama series called *Atlanta*, shared a similar sentiment when I chatted with her in the Eileen Norris Cinema Theatre on February 6, 2020. She expressed very humbly that her life would not be the same without the support of her friends and family, letting me know how lucky she was to be on *Atlanta's* set after waiting tables for a long period of time.

Like musicians and actors, entrepreneurs have to be patient. They also have to be persistent because success will often come when you least expect it. Embracing difficulty like these two creatives is necessary to build character and a portfolio worthy of a successful venture.

THE KIMS

Living through the Third, Fourth, Fifth, and Sixth Republics of South Korea, Haeran Yang and Keehwee Kim endured the uncomfortable continuation of military rule. Determined to create a family together, they dreamed of coming to California to start a business and a new life. Despite being decently well-off in their home country, they knew for their two daughters and son, America would have more options for them. Korea has a very strict education system and a very linear school to career path. The family wanted to see their children thrive socially, academically, and spiritually with more liberties and a better chance at being successful.

When entering the United States, Haeran and Keehwee realized working was an important piece to their ability to stay. After discovering a store called Sushi Lover was going out of business, they bought it with the little money they already had to transform it into a restaurant of their own in June 2013. Eleven years later, I attended school with their daughter and son, Jiho and Bryan Kim, at Archbishop Mitty High School in San Jose. I was able to sit down with Bryan and Jiho to talk about the restaurant their parents built up in an interview. Bryan contributed fervently to this process as he was one of the first who supported and joined the operations team of my nonprofit, Good Samaritans of Silicon Valley.

"[Sushi Lover] was a good and cute name," said Bryan, "so we just kept it as is. Of course, we did change the logo to make it more simplistic and minimalist." The family never did much to grow their customer base either. Because Sushi Lover existed before they bought it, their first customers were the same as the previous Sushi Lover customers. Eventually, they made their own website where people could order, and today they have partnered with food delivery companies DoorDash, Uber Eats, and Grubhub, to adhere to COVID-19 social distancing guidelines.

Amazingly, in Sushi Lover's history, the Kims have never spent any money for exposure and advertising. Because of the quality of their food and service, they retained customers as their reach grew by word of mouth and the occasional Google search.

The Kims' story of restaurant success has been a steep uphill battle but very rewarding. They did not have much of a choice when it came to location, in the middle of a neighborhood and hidden behind a gas station. However, they chose this place because the building was cheap, and a lot of the materials they needed were left behind by the owners before them. As for chefs, many workers have come and gone, and they usually only have Korean workers because the Kims and their manager are more comfortable communicating in Korean. Currently, however, they are incredibly understaffed. Because of this, Mrs. Kim and Mr. Kim are working as kitchen cook and sushi chef respectively.

Despite the hard times, Sushi Lover keeps its customers coming back with good food and good service. Bryan, a worker for the restaurant who has seen his parents persevere to succeed, genuinely thinks they have really high-quality fish and that their food is delicious. He eats their food almost every day but has yet to get tired of it. He was quick to point out that they are also very transparent with their customers. If they have a customer who comes regularly, they will give them lots of stuff on the house and tell them how grateful they are for them.

Sushi Lover serves a mix of traditional Japanese sushi, like sashimi, nigiri, and maki, but they also serve a lot of American sushi-like our special rolls. They have a lot of hot Japanese lunch food like bento boxes and chicken katsu, as well as a few Korean-style dishes like bulgogi and k-chirashi. Of course, they also have a good collection of Asian alcohol. Their menu design revolves around customer demand, material cost, and profit.

Unfortunately, they had to change some old menu items because they were losing more money than they were gaining. They also recently had to increase prices due to inflation and the COVID-19 situation. They manage to pay utility bills simply by hard work, but most of the money they make goes into paying the utility bills, so the profit of business has not been huge lately. Despite this, the Kims have kept a positive attitude and have continued to persevere and win the hearts of their many loyal customers, who come back not only because they enjoy the tasty food and wonderful service, but because they know how hard the family works on a daily basis.

Of course, the Kims are among many other restaurant owners who have struggled to keep their businesses afloat during the pandemic. Just as the Kims' remained solid in the face of adversity, Vivian Ku has also mastered resilience to discover success, according to Star Chefs' positive spotlight of her in the 2021 Los Angeles Rising Stars section. She owns a successful collection of restaurants in the Los Angeles area including Pine and Crane in Silver Lake, and Joy in Highland Park. During the pandemic, she lost customers while still having to pay the landlords and overhead costs of her restaurants. Ku, who could have crumbled as so many other restaurants closed around her, decided to do the opposite: expand.

VIVIAN KU

According to a 2020 Eater Los Angeles article by Cathy Chaplin, Taiwanese breakfast was introduced in the San Gabriel Valley a few years prior to the pandemic, with popular spots Yi Mei Deli, Four Sea Restaurant, and Huge Tree Pastry. However, it never entered central Los Angeles until Ku took the initiative in 2020. She opened a new pop-up restaurant called Today Starts Here, serving delectable and classic Taiwanese breakfast treats in Chinatown. The pop-up restaurant operated out of a 1,500 square-foot space that used to be occupied by New Dragon Seafood Restaurant. Menu items included what Ku loves to eat herself, like daikon rice cakes, deep fried crullers, and soy milk.

Despite the road map being unclear, with no outdoor dining at her restaurant Joy, and continuous debates about protocols, Ku opened a pop-up breakfast spot called Today Starts Here, in one of the most COVID-19 infested cities in the world—Los Angeles. Ku says February 2020 was an exciting month as she was planning on opening her third restaurant while hoping to open up potentially two more. She negotiated aggressively with the landlord to bring down the cost of rent, and this allowed her to create a pop-up restaurant in Chinatown while promoting some staff she was planning on promoting (Chaplin, Eater Los Angeles).

By taking a risk, she learned so much because of the ability to experience more than a usual Brick & Mortar restaurant. It was her personal passion project to undertake a creative way to serve people who craved quality food.

Ku did not expect her passion project to be slammed with customers from day one, but it was. Today Starts Here started the day for many Los Angelenos. Eater LA sat down with Ku to interview her on her success to publish in their 2020 article because of her bold resilience during such a downtrodden, pandemic ridden year within the restaurant industry. Ku, incredibly, was able to operate three restaurants at once during a time when many could not even handle one.

Ku is inspired by sharing her Taiwanese culture through her food, and a lot of the joy she extracts from her job is seeing her customers grow empathetically warm to the aspects surrounding the food: the language, the shared East Asian values, and the calming, appreciative ambiance. Ku knew she wanted to open a restaurant because she liked the energy and how it brought people together so magically. Taiwanese food made sense for her because it is so underrepresented but has so much to offer. On a *How I Built This with Guy Raz* podcast episode during a Resilience Series, Ku explained, "Taiwanese food is organically designed to appeal to the masses because of the way history and migration shaped its culinary history."

Within the podcast, Ku explained how she grew up in Bakersfield, California, where her family had moved for the agriculture industry. Her father bought a farm when she was young, and she grew up planting seeds. She witnessed how they ran a small business and responded in moments of difficulty.

After studying sustainable agriculture, food systems, and agribusiness at Harvard University, Ku chose to work in the restaurant industry because she loved the creativity, the happiness of going out in public and bringing people together. Ku's biggest inspiration is her grandfather, a man of principle. He told her, "There are no inferior jobs, only inferior people. It doesn't matter what you do, but how you do it." She understands the situation at hand never matters as much as the response to that situation (Guy Raz, Podcast).

The main obstacle to her was always fear of failure. She borrowed money from her parents, aunts, and boyfriend to go to culinary school because she did not want to be in debt to a bank. Money was always in the back of her mind, as it is for many young restaurateurs. She also had a lot of hesitancy when deciding to sign a lease for a restaurant, but the thought of being in the restaurant industry for the rest of her life, pursuing what she loved, pushed her to take a risk (Guy Raz, Podcast).

Ku had many ups and downs trying to keep staff above water, as she did not make the PPP loan the first round. But she was in a sector that is both price point and take-out friendly, which helped her maintain business, as opposed to bars and fine-dining establishments. She had to close her restaurants for two months, and when she opened back up, people were excited and generous with their tips. During the summer of 2020, Ku said she had to check in with her staff daily, ensuring they were healthy and safe. She knew she had to stay open for the community and the longevity of her restaurants (Guy Raz, Podcast).

What were initially extremely high-pressure situations, pushing the employees to come together to make important decisions, have turned into hope and a light at the end of the tunnel. Ku declared once you understand and trust both the back of the house and front of the house, anything is possible!

Ku is an example of the reward that comes from embracing adversity and continuing to do what you love. The fact that she has seen herself through such an economic downturn gives her extreme confidence for her future in the food business. Her empowering story of embracing one's mission, even if it may be difficult, parallels the persistent vision the Kims pursued during their turbulent first few years in the business that eventually turned into major success and happiness for their whole family.

Both the Kims and Ku represent stories of perseverance in the restaurant business. There are many ways to overcome adversity: rebrand, hire different people, improve the well-being within your restaurant, or embrace your heritage and who you are deep down. When the going gets tough, you must push through to achieve what you initially wanted. Sometimes, it won't be easy to realize your potential when so much seems to be riding against you. However, it is in this moment that an adjustment, a pivot, or a shot in the dark of Red Bull vodka will push you to newer heights you never thought of before.

Both the Kims and Ku have reached levels of success they never thought they would achieve simply because both went forward with grit and dynamism, letting no one get in the way of their achieving the visions of who they wanted to become or what they desired their brand to reach. The most successful restaurants in the fine-dining restaurant space have owners and chefs who are exuberant, opinionated, bold, confident, and in tune with their people. While embracing adversity, it is easier to embrace who you are, which aids significantly in finding a new career plateau.

CHAPTER 12

FOLLOW YOUR PASSION UNAPOLOGETICALLY

———

"Life is either a daring adventure or
nothing at all."

—HELEN KELLER

Speaking with Ben Rosenthal, a critical component of the
press and social media team at Eleven Madison Park, it is
clear that head chef, owner, and visionary, Daniel Humm is
overloaded with work as he turns what has been called the
greatest restaurant in the world completely vegan. According to his gripping episode on *How I Built This with Guy
Raz*, the superstar chef dropped out of school at age fourteen
and became a father at age eighteen. It was a combination
that could cause anyone to forfeit a lucrative professional
career. However, cyclist Daniel Humm had a different plan
for his life, one where he was going to outwork everyone
around him.

In the podcast, Humm expressed how he dreamed of becoming a competitive cyclist and how he supported himself initially by cutting vegetables and making soup stock at fine restaurants in Switzerland. Today, Humm is considered one of the greatest chefs in the world, owning the acclaimed restaurant Eleven Madison Park in New York City. In any aspect of life, it is not about where you start but where you finish.

When speaking to Jerry West, an NBA Executive and the current NBA logo, through a Zoom screen at The Lorenzo (an apartment complex in South Central), I realized that passion can be life-saving. The NBA legend remarked that the only thing that made him happy were his passions: fishing and basketball. Otherwise, he was alone most of the time and disliked himself. The man suffered from severe depression and basketball became his life and allowed him to create a name for himself.

Several aspiring chefs, restaurant owners, or entrepreneurs may be in a poor place in their lives or feel down on their luck due to multiple setbacks or life circumstances. The only thing you can control, however, is how you respond. Like Humm and West, success and purpose were found through following passions without any regard for the people beside them in their respective fields or industries. Passions and well-being go hand in hand.

When speaking with the Director of Belonging at USC, Cat Moore, she explains how a sense of belonging and a sense of purpose go hand in hand. Once she found her passion at USC herself through the encouragement of a physics professor, she found her footing and was able to be her genuine self and grow to her potential. Following your passions and reaching one's potential go hand in hand, especially in the world of entrepreneurship.

In his talk with Guy Raz, Humm shared that he learned about food at a young age, declaring, "My mom was half French and half Italian—the importance of the best ingredients from farms and washing lettuce." His dad was an architect, and this combination meant that cooking was an art form at home that only featured the best ingredients possible. His mom cooked elegantly, and both his parents appreciated simplicity and attention to detail in their lives, including their food. He grew up humbly, only eating meat on the weekends. On the rare occasion that his family would eat meat together, they would use and cherish every single part. This mindset meant even using the bones to make soup.

Humm felt like nothing he did was ever good enough for his parents, from school work to chores to sports, from a young age. He even won nationals twice in cross country but felt he received no love or respect from his family. Because he never felt welcome at his family's home, he moved in with his girlfriend when he was fifteen. Life with his girlfriend was a "simple but beautiful existence." When Humm was eighteen, he and his girlfriend decided to foster a baby, forcing Humm to grow up quickly. He figured out that few people have a career in cycling, but at the same time, Humm was falling in love with the process of creating food. He witnessed chefs working so precisely, calmly, and beautifully. He decided to rise to the top in cooking rather than cycling, so cooking became his new sport (Guy Raz, Podcast).

After running cross country, he discovered the thrill of bike riding. He would get up at 4 a.m. and energetically ride to the French part of Switzerland. He would be gone for hours as the sport was his escape from home. When he was fourteen years old, he could join a team, so he left school to compete professionally full time. In total, he only went to school for eight years. Because of his lack of cash, Humm was forced to work in the restaurant industry purely for the money at first. Fortunately, he received his first job because the chef who interviewed him also loved cycling. This chef taught him how to make a consommé, butcher a chicken, and produce the chicken stock. Humm knew he felt right at home in the kitchen early on but never thought of making it a career (Guy Raz, Podcast).

Humm began his cooking career at a humble restaurant serving Swiss food in the Alps, preparing honest, simple dishes from ingredients shipped in from local farms. Plates included veal, liver, and tripe, but Humm started cooking special dinners, not on the menu. After six months, he received a Michelin star at the age of twenty-four. Humm was often overwhelmed and stressed serving the Swiss locals every day, who grew to love his amazing food. These stressful nights allowed Humm to flourish when he came to America. When he was only twenty-five, the relationship with his daughter's mother ended, and he moved to the United States because it was too painful to be in Zurich (Guy Raz, Podcast).

Becoming a chef in the US was an incredibly intense environment. His coworkers and bosses were aggressive and competitive, and many people did not want others to succeed. Humm worked with a chef who asked him to count every pea, and if there was one missing before preparing the main dish, there were severe consequences. In the beginning, Humm desired to learn parts of the craft such as knife cutting, making sauces, and butchering the fish. He wanted to become the cleanest and quickest chef in the world. He started to draw imaginary dishes, creating outrageous entrées in his head, and he frequently referenced a quote from Miles Davis: "You have to learn the rules before you can break them." He humbly reminded himself he needed to learn the ropes before branching out (Guy Raz, Podcast).

Humm set his sights on Northern California to become the executive chef at Campton Place. Humm arrived in San Francisco in 2003 at twenty-seven years old, and everything felt foreign. This difficulty was due to his attachment to the New York way of life. It took him a while to live like a Californian in a hilly land with more warm personalities around him. He immediately met Alice Waters, owner of Chez Panisse and probably the most famous chef in California, at the French Laundry. He desired to establish himself and receive vital advice.

According to a 2005 San Francisco Rising Stars article, posted by Star Chefs, he worked at Campton Place, where critics would regularly check out the updates and what was going on. Humm found his stride at the restaurant, seeing his dreams come to life before his eyes. A few years after Humm's arrival, the article points out that the notable food critic Michael Bower called the acclaimed chef "the brightest star to last in Northern California since Thomas Keller opened up the French Laundry."

Humm lived every day like it was a competition. He knew he wanted to be a great chef, and he did not let anything stand in his way.

When Raz asked Humm about the landscape of the industry, he acknowledged that resources are limited as chefs grow and come up because they do not have the most significant budget. It is often very overwhelming, and many, including chef Humm, usually do not know how to get to the end of the day. Many workers think about several ideas that were also going through Humm's active mind: promotion, training duration, and ability to learn and grow without being overworked. Humm admitted that it took such a big commitment, and he knew he needed to trust the management team of Campton Place.

Three years after moving to California, Humm moved back to New York City to become executive chef of Eleven Madison Park. Humm admits that one of the hardest things he's ever done is pleasing customers in New York City because the change was incredibly hard. However, his passion for success and his concept pushed him through. One can only be successful if one manages their business. In other words, you can only continue being a restaurant chef if you make money. Humm recognized that hospitality is arguably more important than even food. He stated, "People come for the food, but hospitality makes guests return and return" (Guy Raz, Podcast).

This sentiment means that passion must be toward your concept and marketability as much as your food quality to make sure it is funneled in the most productive way possible.

In September 2008, Lehman Brothers collapsed, and Eleven Madison Park struggled significantly. Humm put it in his team's head to produce a clear path to move from three stars to four stars in the *New York Times* restaurant reviews. Because of this goal, Humm operated on high expenses, meaning that they served on a four-star level but didn't necessarily charge on a four-star level. Humm admits that they had nights where they only had four guests in the restaurant.

He went as far as inviting friends and others to make the restaurant look packed. This thinking was just one of the many tricks that Eleven Madison Park employed to impress reviewers (Guy Raz, Podcast).

In August 2009, the restaurant received a glowing review in the *New York Times* from Frank Bruni titled "A Daring Rise to The Top." Humm admits he has not had an empty seat since, due to their attention to detail. They accepted that star they were craving and the label from Bruni as the "most alluring and impressive in New York."

Humm was so determined to be successful he created an algorithm for dishes to ensure they were of the highest quality. Art guided his creating process, but he has consistently refined his strategy for years. Humm likes to cook with very few ingredients that say a lot. He makes sure they meet four critical criteria for all of his dishes. First, the dish has to be instantaneously delicious without a thought. Second, the dish has to be beautiful. Third, the dish must be creative by moving food forward with new flavor combinations. Last, the dish must be intentional, encapsulating a childhood memory, featuring ingredients grown together, or spotlighting another artist. For example, the halibut he prepares is served with pickled daikon on top of many multicolored radishes. It is a vibrant and unique dish with orange blossom sauce on the side (Guy Raz, Podcast).

Eleven Madison Park was on the World's 50 Best Restaurants for ten consecutive years and eventually became number one in 2017. He and his cofounder, Will Guidara, would push harder to reach the summit every year. However, the moment they received number one was not the most significant moment of their life, Humm admits in the Guy Raz podcast. This difference was because they had nothing to look forward to once they hit number one, which significantly impacted their synergy and togetherness. They thought that going separate ways may be the best option, but Humm remained persistent and bought Eleven Madison Park.

Humm wanted to win by creating the best experience for his customers, but it became difficult to fit everything in. It is harder to measure accomplishments when you are pulled in many different directions. There are always so many attractive directions when one is an executive chef. Having time for a personal life became challenging for him and his relationships. After reflecting on his dramatic rise to the top, Humm reflected, "If a chef is loud and yelling, he is weak and overwhelmed" (Guy Raz, Podcast).

To embrace his skills, Humm decided to go to soup kitchens where volunteers were consistently leaving because most were elderly. He knew his kitchen was empty and wanted to help with the food insecurity problem. So, the chef started producing meals just two weeks after the restaurant closed and went into neighborhoods to give away food. This endeavor exposed him to parts of NYC he did not know. He admits he was "looking into people's eyes, and people were full of fear." This activity allowed him to reconnect with a part of food he was not familiar with anymore. That empowering part was human connection and generosity. He connected with food in a new way, cooking over one million meals since March 2020. During this time, he even faced bankruptcy and had to sell his house to figure it out and refinance (Guy Raz, Podcast).

In the podcast, a quote that Humm often returns to in his extraordinary life of commitment is, "Life is either a daring adventure or nothing at all." Humm, who is an avid biker and runner, has a life motto very similar to mine: "All gas no brake." His motto reminds him of when he moved to America with two suitcases. He knows he will not cook meals for people in need. So, this year, he committed that part of the price of reservations will go to people in need.

Quarantining has caused Humm to be more aware of his surroundings: the way Americans consume food and how some food sources are ruining the world. He decided that Eleven Madison Park would become entirely plant-based, but Humm declares, "The change will be in some ways subtle." After the meal, he wants people to discover that they cannot believe they did not eat butter or cream. He has dreamed up mouth-watering moments with just vegetables.

For example, a stock of combo and mushroom roasted deeper, so stock caramelizes around the mushroom. Then incorporate pine needles and mushroom powder because he wants meat-eaters to be blown away by vegetables. Humm always loves challenges, saying, "To see the creativity of a chef is to see them work with vegetables." A momentous decision for Eleven Madison Park came on June 10, when they reopened for dining, after being closed a year, with an entirely plant-based menu. This change is the equivalent of Tom Brady or Aaron Rogers leaving the NFL to play flag football. Out of the 100 Michelin-star restaurants on earth, none is vegan (Guy Raz, Podcast).

Humm also wants to push the envelope by making time a new ingredient. This phenomenon means utilizing time to create and open up new flavors. Sometimes the longer a pot sits or, the longer a drink ferments, the better it may taste.

So Humm wants to explore this concept of time concerning his vegetarian concoctions (Guy Raz, Podcast).

When Humm was in elementary school, his teacher asked all the students to draw a house on paper. Humm could not do the task because the paper was not big enough. Instead, he drew a considerable place that used his paper and all the other desks in the room as a canvas, and the teacher made him go to therapy. Humm talks about his passion often, specifically "leidenschaft" which means deep passion that often comes with pain. Humm's extremely competitive nature feeds into his passion which feeds into a life of success that covers up his many strong emotions and failures (Guy Raz, Podcast).

As an entrepreneur, and more importantly, as a leader who people respect and listen to, having passion is heavily required. Humm's story is the epitome of passion because he continuously pushed to be the best in his field, whether biking, running, or cooking and leading staff. To run a fine-dining establishment, one must exhibit an extreme passion for their concept and restaurant because enthusiasm, understanding, and inspiration are needed to have customers returning for more. Passion means one cares deeply about something, and that care equates to more intentional time and energy in the right directions.

CHAPTER 13

THE PANDEMIC

"If you aren't nervous about your passion,
you aren't passionate about it."

—BOBBY FLAY

I was staying in the JW Marriott Los Angeles Live presidential suite, performing some staff calls to my Wells Fargo employees based in Manhattan. It was one of my last days with the company before I started my senior year of college. I invited my dad to come to Bestia with me after hearing some positive buzz around town and from a mentor in New York City. The experience was exquisite. My father and I enjoyed their Margarita and Spicy Lamb Sausage pizzas, along with their Saffron Gnocchi and Squid Ink Chitarra.

"The whole point of restaurants is they're places to let go of the stress of your everyday life. As long as this virus is rampant and deadly, people aren't going to be able to fully relax in a restaurant. I want our restaurant to be an escape." This remark is what Pastry Chef Genevieve Gergis, who owns famed Italian restaurant Bestia with her husband and Executive

Chef Ori Menashe, told *Los Angeles Magazine* in 2020. After my frequent visits in the fall of 2021, the bartender and the hostesses referred me to the power couple and the PR team.

According to a 2020 *Los Angeles Magazine* article by Andy Wang, the pair own and operate two of the most successful fine-dining restaurants in Los Angeles: Bestia ("Beast" in Italian) and Bavel. Gergis and Menashe met in 2005 at Gino Angelini's La Terza where Menashe was a cook and Gergis was a hostess. In 2012, the couple transformed LA's Arts District when they opened a small dish, rustic yet modern, concept that left locals speechless. People from all over Los Angeles county were swarming the industrial Arts District for the best Italian food in the city. Then, in 2018, the unstoppable duo opened Bavel, which quickly became a sensation, serving Middle Eastern food such as hummus masabacha, grilled prawns, slow-roasted lamb neck shawarma, and lavender labneh tulumba churros.

Despite their popularity, and undeniable, next-level concepts, Bestia and Bavel struggled when COVID-19 hit. The fact is that the restaurant business has very slim margins, which means it relies on high volumes of customers; even the best restaurants have a minimal financial cushion (Wang, *LA Magazine*).

According to the interview with the pair, included in Wang's article, when the pandemic wreaked havoc on Los Angeles, one of the most affected cities in the country, Gergis and Menashe considered closing down entirely due to their financial troubles. Gergis explained her accountant told her they'd be bankrupt by May 1, 2020. They were left with about $100,000, paying $65,000 a month for health insurance and other overhead costs. That left them with two ultimate options: shut everything down completely and give up all of their employees' life insurance or sell as many to-go orders as they could so they could maintain their employees' health insurance while also attempting to pay off some of the utility and rent bills.

They decided to offer a full takeout service to get their delicious dishes to hungry and loyal customers. However, during much of 2020, this consisted of selling out two hundred orders at each restaurant, which usually hit at least five hundred dinners a night before the pandemic. The main thing that kept the pair alive during this turbulent period was their loving customers. Several customers bought extra merchandise and gift cards (one even purchased a five-thousand-dollar gift card). Many Los Angelenos love their restaurants and designate a reservation as an exciting portion of their social life. There is nothing like starting the night at a fine-dining establishment, and the community support for both Bestia and Bavel was instrumental in keeping them afloat (Wang, *LA Magazine*).

Incredibly, both Bestia and Bavel experienced zero cases of the virus among their employees, which caused significant challenges for several other Los Angeles restaurants.

The owners eventually stopped takeout in the middle of summer 2020 because of the trained professionals they hire to create their elite dining experience, known for finishing their fresh meals seconds before it is placed in front of a hungry customer. They knew the city would open up soon, so they stopped takeout completely with hopes that they could return to the environment that made them famous. Bestia and Bavel both reopened for outdoor dining on July 7, 2020 (Wang, *LA Magazine*).

Both restaurants reopened with different menus. Of course, the classics remained, but several other dishes were taken off and replaced by new concepts. Gergis was very disappointed with how Los Angeles handled the virus, not warning restaurateurs about the longevity and lasting effects. People, especially owners, had alarming rates of anxiety and stress due to Los Angeles' lack of proper leadership to calm down the city. Gergis would stay up late and have nightmares about employees who might not get enough to eat or have the proper nutrition to supplement their food. This haunting mindset partly inspired her creation of Feed Love LA, a nonprofit that feeds restaurant workers (Wang, *LA Magazine*).

However, Gergis thinks that the pandemic has allowed people to see the positive side of their lives and enjoy the fact they even get to go out to restaurants to take a break from their regular lives.

HOW OTHER LOS ANGELES RESTAURANTS WEATHERED THE PANDEMIC

It was September of 2021, and I decided to take my mother out to JOEY DTLA, who was in town for the weekend. After a light lunch at Zinqué featuring salmon toast and a quinoa breakfast burrito, I wanted to treat my mother to a more filling meal at a restaurant known for its globally inspired menu. We sat down at JOEY and enjoyed exquisitely prepared Tuna & Avocado roll, Seared Salmon roll, Yellowfin Tuna salad, and my favorite cocktail, a Moscow mule.

According to their website, JOEY Restaurants, a host of popular destinations throughout the United States and Canada, has three Los Angeles locations: Downtown, Manhattan Beach, and Woodland Hills. JOEY offers a unique experience similar to Bestia and Bavel due to its modern and internationally inspired cuisine. The environment creates an authentic and lively ambiance, with incredibly fresh food, an open kitchen, a lounge, and an aesthetically industrial dining room. Each newcomer to JOEY enjoys a glass of champagne and a warm introduction to their diverse sushi menu, sandwiches, burgers, salads, fish, and steak. After speaking with the hostess and indirectly with head chef Jordan Senger, I gleaned that when the pandemic hit, JOEY offered many alternatives to indoor dining, including JOEY at home, meal kits, cocktail kits, gift boxes, and alcohol like liquor, beer, and wine.

The Los Angeles community rallied around JOEY and enabled it to overcome the effects of having to close in-person dining.

When reopening became plausible, JOEY established a page on their website to educate customers on safety guidelines and the best way to reopen without any more hazardous hiccups. This page included a thank you note to loyal customers who helped them by buying to-go orders and different kits throughout the pandemic. It also had plans for each of its locations in the US and Canada, so customers would know what restaurants were fully open and available exclusively outdoors, among other safety guidelines.

Restaurants that have been transparent and proactive about these health guidelines have retained their customers and survived the pandemic and will most likely continue to do so as COVID-19 persists. According to JOEY Restaurants website, in their Canadian locations, Vaccine Passports are required for entrance, and all sites in Seattle and Los Angeles are open indoors and on the patio without a six-foot distancing rule anymore. All Canadian restaurants still have the six-foot distancing rule. They also included a large section about the implemented protocols to ensure the health and safety of all their customers and employees. Some of these protocols include QR codes for guests to access the menu via personal cell phones, and new training given to employees to ensure they can handle their safety and the guests' safety.

The pandemic brought a thick air of anxiety to the streets of Beverly Hills, causing many small businesses to be hesitant to serve their customers or be guarded in continuing their business. The *Beverly Hills Courier*, the local media outlet, reached out to many restaurants during the pandemic to see how they were persevering through such a challenging period. One massive concept in the city that kept foot traffic alive was the parklet, or a small seating area that created a public space on or along a sidewalk.

According to a 2020 article posted by the *Beverly Hills Courier*, there are over eighteen parklets throughout the city as many were built in 2020 to accommodate businesses needing to move their operations outside. The Open BH initiative, which helped over ninety-one small businesses in Beverly Hills move business to sidewalks or parking lots during 2020, loved the idea of creating more parklets. So, they dedicated funds and resources to help companies relocate to available parklets, which pleased Los Angeles restaurant-goers who could sit and enjoy the nice weather while eating their favorite meals.

Urth Caffé, the popular casual European-style café with no waiters, took advantage of the parklet. Shallom Berkman, the owner of Urth Caffé on South Beverly Drive, said social distancing caused a reduction in their tables from one hundred to fourteen. However, because of the city's generosity, they could expand their seating area into the parklet. In March 2020, Berkman and his team launched a preorder and delivery site that became a massive part of business throughout 2020 and generated a lot of revenue. Looking back, Berkman is proud of what he and his team accomplished in such a short period to stay afloat (Dixon, Beverly Hills Courier).

Allessandro Jacchia was a newcomer to Beverly Hills, opening his gelato restaurant, Fatamorgana Gelato, on Beverly Drive. Jacchia witnessed over thirty places go up for lease just in 2020 on South Beverly Drive from Wilshire Boulevard to Olympic Boulevard, including every type of store from retail to coffee shops to fine-dining establishments. Jacchia established his restaurant as a dessert staple for locals despite the harsh circumstances. Since it opened, Fatamorgana Gelato has served over sixty-six gelato flavors with twenty-four incredible vegan flavors. Jacchia seems to be doing something right because his store is one of very few that stayed open throughout the entirety of the pandemic except for a few days due to riots (Dixon, Beverly Hills Courier).

Despite limited capacity, Jacchia was able to stay afloat due to the demand for his product. He was already considering expansion, and now that COVID-19 protocols are starting to pull back, there is not much stopping him. He also operates cloud kitchens in Koreatown, Downtown LA, and Hollywood. A cloud kitchen, known as a "ghost kitchen" or a "virtual kitchen," is a cooking facility set up exclusively for delivery only meals. This setup means that there is no storefront seating for customers. Jacchia believes that the future of the restaurant industry may be in cloud kitchens where customers do not have to sit on a sidewalk to enjoy fine-dining food while paying three hundred dollars for service. His prediction is supported by the numerous pop-up, takeout, or food truck eateries that have been successfully serving delicious food recently (Dixon, Beverly Hills Courier).

PERMANENT CLOSURES

Due to the pandemic, there have been several permanent closures of restaurants in Los Angeles that have come to define their communities with their unique concepts, lively ambiance, and impeccable food combinations. *Los Angeles Magazine* published a holistic article in January 2021 titled "An Ever-Growing List of LA Restaurants That Have Closed Amid the Pandemic."

In Downtown Los Angeles, several classic restaurants all shut down. Restaurants such as:

- Preux & Proper (Josh Kopel's Southern Cuisine Restaurant)
- Plum Tree Inn (one of many Chinatown destinations going under)
- Bon Temps (Lincoln Carson's Arts District Concept)
- Terroni DTLA (only Beverly location is open)
- Patina (Joachim Splichal's elegant French concept)
- Broken Spanish (Ray Garcia's modern Mexican concept)
- Bad Son Tacos (fresh taco joint)
- Bäco Mercat (Josef Centeno's Spanish-fusion restaurant)

According to *Los Angeles Magazine*, the financial pressures of the pandemic forced established chefs to forgo some of their best concepts to avoid bankruptcy and losing everything. Many top restaurants in Downtown Los Angeles had to call it quits. It was not just downtown that faced hardship. Beverly Hills and Hollywood saw some of their flagship restaurants sink as well.

According to a 2020 article posted by *Today*, in Beverly Hills, Lisa Vanderpump's Villa Blanca, her first ever restaurant, could not sustain the star power of her other restaurants. Unfortunately, Vanderpump and her husband, Ken Todd, had to make the tough decision to close because their landlord would not renegotiate their lease. Vanderpump is now focused on her other restaurants but remains optimistic that she will reopen Villa Blanca at another location one day. Roxbury Café was another famous spot that could not survive the COVID-19 pandemic.

The casual café was known for its classic Italian and American food with vegetarian-friendly salads that many nurses and doctors would visit from the nearby health facilities. This was only eight years after I was sitting at a table next to her at the now closed Beverly Hills Fleming's Steakhouse location, overhearing her and her reality TV costar discussing the excitement around the restaurant. I was in town for the 2013 Rose Bowl football game on New Year's Day between Stanford and Wisconsin (*Today*, 2020).

In West Hollywood, Aburiya Raku, known for its charcoal-grilled skewers of both meat and vegetables, closed down due to financial troubles. Locals will miss its sake list and all the chalkboard specials which feature fresh seafood combinations. In East Hollywood, Wah's Golden Hen closed after fifty years of serving Chinese takeout in Virgil Village. Owner Lena Louie posted a goodbye on Yelp, explaining that she can now enjoy a quiet retirement of cooking with family and gardening at home (*LA Magazine*, 2021).

According to the 2021 article, other popular restaurants in Hollywood that closed included 101 Coffee Shop (diner and film spot), Auburn (Eric Bost's fine-dining concept), The Pikey (British pub), and Trois Mec (the Michelin-star phenomenon). In Los Angeles, one of the best cities in the world for fine dining, it is clear to see the struggles every restaurateur had to face during the pandemic. Los Angeles' challenges reflected those of many cities throughout the world, and at the brink of 2022, some restaurants were just starting to recover from their financial losses. Other restaurateurs and chefs decided to take advantage of the circumstances and retire like Lena Louie did.

The restaurant industry in Los Angeles and the rest of the world will never be the same, but it remains resilient by evolving and adapting. It's a new world, but we still have to eat.

Several of my favorite restaurants have thankfully weathered the pandemic positively, while others have unfortunately been forced to shut their doors for good. Based on the restaurants that have survived, the traits of successful owners are traits we have returned to repeatedly: flexibility, adaptability, and perseverance in the face of the unknown. The example of chefs' will and ability to entrepreneurially pivot to survive throughout the pandemic will help restaurateurs and chefs hone their problem-solving skills. It is fair to say that it is only up from here for restaurateurs. The pandemic will provide a moment in time for business analysts and hustling entrepreneurs to study to overcome their future issues, whether it be getting through another shutdown or simply dealing with a changing restaurant climate.

Ultimately, the pandemic has taught the start-up world that practically anything can happen. It reminded us that life as an entrepreneur is bumpy and unpredictable, warranting a mindset that makes no assumptions and has no expectations, but gives 110 percent every day. In the fine-dining restaurant industry, in particular, an entrepreneur must be ready to go against what they thought yesterday to be successful ultimately. The world changes so fast, and to continue to be successful yourself, you must continually evolve and change with it. This evolution may mean closing one location to focus on another or revamping the menu completely to create higher profit margins due to lower costs. In start-ups I have had the pleasure of working for, I have earned the name of "jackrabbit" because of how fast I move. This fast-moving quality is essential to create a winning recipe for your team and, more importantly, to become stronger when hardship comes your way, like the pandemic.

CHAPTER 14

CLOSING REMARKS: TASTE EACH BITE

"Pull up a chair. Take a taste. Come join us. Life is so endlessly delicious."

—RUTH REICHL

The development of the restaurant industry would be nonexistent if it were not for one human trait that we often take for granted in our lives: our sense of taste. Taste is a concept that allows us to enjoy the pleasure of flavor combinations that bring us back to our childhood or transport us overseas to Sicily, Greece, or Bangkok. One of our many senses that allows us to find pleasure in providing nutrients for our body. So, the primary question is, how do we develop our sense of taste?

Arguably, an essential aspect of our sense of taste is our tongue. According to a Heather Hatfield article, "The Science Behind How We Taste" posted on WebMD, our tongue is sensitive to many tastes, from sweet and sour, to bitter and salty. Incredibly, taste comes from more than simply the taste buds within your mouth. Taste is a complex combination of food smells, looks, and sounds. It feeds off all our other senses to build its end product. Ultimately, taste is a product of our genes, environment, and age.

As with many human traits, genes give us predetermined taste buds that establish our initial preference for different foods. Our choices come down to how our receptors react to different tastes. For example, while your friend may enjoy coffee, you may not because you might have fewer bitter receptors to enjoy the whole experience coffee's authentic taste can offer. Experience in tasting is also a critical part of life to understand how to push your boundaries and find your valid preferences. Training taste is possible through learning. We cannot change our genes, so some preferences are hard to transform, but with more exposure to foods comes a better chance of decreasing your intense dislikes and increasing your likes. For instance, someone who continues to drink coffee every day despite their disliking it, can develop a fondness for it over time. (Hatfield, WebMD).

Hatfield also explains that besides sweet, sour, bitter, and salty, scientists have found a fifth taste called umami which describes the taste of glutamate, an amino acid in many protein-rich foods such as animal meat. This taste is often associated with savory, brothy, and meaty sensations. Umami has been part of Japanese cuisine for a hundred years and is now a vital part of taste for many eaters worldwide.

It is also essential to distinguish between flavor and taste. Flavor has as much to do with scent as it does with your mouth and bite. The distinctive flavor of your dish comes from its aroma and taste. The airway we have between our nose and mouth allows us to put together the incredible smell of a dish and the five distinct tastes of a dish to create endless combinations of enjoyable flavors (Hatfield, WebMD).

Given this knowledge, the flavor combinations a chef can come up with are almost endless. This fact is why a restaurateur must understand the ambiance, the smell, the lighting, the textures of the seats and walls, and the presentation of the food all come together in the customer's mind to create a tasting experience. This tasting experience has the power to change a person's life. This transformative experience inspires chefs to develop cutting-edge concepts that offer a game-changing experience for food lovers looking for another escape. Whether it be piña coladas on the coast of Bora Bora or blue cheese gnocchi on a boat in Venice, the sensory impact creates a lively flavor that undoubtedly keeps us coming back for every game-changing fine-dining meal.

When opening a restaurant, follow your heart. As stated in Katherine LaGrave's exquisite 2019 *Vogue* article, chef Christina Nguyen finally built up the courage to represent her heritage when she opened up a Vietnamese restaurant, Hai Hai, to recreate dishes she ate when she was growing up: true authentic South Asian food. When exploring her aesthetically pleasing and peaceful website, a customer can recognize that rather than simply Pad Thai or pho, which have now become popularized in American cuisine, Nguyen shines the spotlight on dishes that many people do not know. It took the James Beard Finalist some time to finally show off her roots, but it has paid off. Her story and many others throughout history illustrate the power of bringing oneself into the concept to create something that is part of you. For

Nguyen's loyal customers, it is easy to see the vibrancy and connectedness she has with each dish that is served.

Every aspect matters when dreaming up a delicious vision to serve your local community, and as long as each box is checked with confidence, then there is almost nothing holding you back, except the need for passion and hiring the right people. Finding this united team of optimists and believers also has to do with the hiring process, which should be entirely holistic. Rather than hiring someone based on experience, the restaurant owner should hire people who just desire to work for them because they love the restaurant's concept and mission and want to be proponents of it. This type of hiring will allow for one to build a team of trusted and passionate individuals who can support one another while handling their own responsibilities.

The American diet is a funny being. I reference it as a being because it changes as a human changes and is very unpredictable. There is no limit to the creativity one can have in their restaurant concept. What is important, however, is recognizing the trend of people in the city in which you plan to open your restaurant. For example, some cities, such as Los Angeles, have a growing vegan population, and nationwide, health is starting to matter a lot more, especially when it comes to food. When thinking of a restaurant concept, keep this in the back of your mind because one should not try to pull Americans attempting to be healthier back into a pit of greasy saturated fats and processed carbohydrates. Include vegan and vegetarian options on the menu and denote this somehow with a leaf icon to let your healthy customers know what adheres to their diet.

According to a 2021 *Wall Street Journal* article posted online by Adam Davidson, David Humm recognized this change in the American diet, and he boldly transformed his Michelin-three-starred Eleven Madison Park into an entirely meatless concept. Humm, now famous in New York for having one of the best restaurants in the world, is fascinatingly creating an almost entirely vegan menu. Many elite chefs are following in Humm's bold footsteps, creating tasty vegetarian dishes to serve their customers. Thankfully, Americans can still enjoy fine dining while staying slim, and this trend seems to be increasing.

***

Opening a restaurant is not a walk in the park or a walk in the kitchen. Instead, it takes strategy, grit, perseverance, but most of all, passion in your concept and vision. Restaurateurs take years to build the courage to open their establishment and be the leader and head chef of a fine-dining place. The training a chef gets, whether overseas at top-rated restaurants or working for an already established friend's restaurant in the US, is critical to building confidence and the skills to become independent.

An aspiring restaurant owner needs to think critically about the location, the chef, and the menu behind their concept. Every piece of the puzzle matters because the difference between a thriving restaurant and a struggling restaurant can often be very slim, like a particular dish or a prime spot on the corner of a busy intersection by the beach.

An aspiring entrepreneur needs to inspire their employees by encouraging and promoting positive reinforcement. Positivity and passion are contagious, and in the restaurant industry, where things can go wrong almost daily, positivity is necessary not to allow this mishap to steamroll into many issues or a cloud of negativity.

But most importantly, follow your heart. Your restaurant concept will only ever be as strong as your investment in the project. An owner or chef with a clear and personal vision will attract the attention of employees, customers, and critics. As a restaurateur or an aspiring entrepreneur, it is critical to utilize your drive, authenticity, and genuine care for the product to allow it to blossom. The most successful restaurateurs and entrepreneurs I have met in my twenty-one years of life on earth seem to have one thing in common: a stubborn need to show the world who they are and their value proposition to the world. Each and every one was unique. But they were special because they were persistent, passionate, and purpose-led.

BONUS CONTENT

"Life is a series of commas, not periods."

—MATTHEW MCCONAUGHEY

EXCLUSIVE DINING EXPERIENCE: MICHELIN CONTENDER, FELLOW (TARA ELAINE BRENNAN, PHILLIP CAMINO, AND ME)

It is Friday, February 25, 2022, and I finish up a string of meetings with my adviser, my partner at Screen360tv, and some dear family members. Chef Philip Camino, CEO and founder of Camino Industries, was awaiting Tara Brennen and me for a 5 p.m. dinner at one of the excellent restaurants he heavily focuses on: the modern American hotspot located in West Los Angeles called Fellow.

I drove from my house in South Central to the beautiful area of Westwood, the neighborhood of Fellow. I walked down the lit-up Glendon Avenue, just beginning to catch some buzz on a warm Friday night. I walked through thick hanging drapes into a gallery housing gorgeous modern art featuring up-and-coming artists. Then, I turned left into a spacious room that was dimly lit, and brightly colored with paintings that complemented each other powerfully, building a chic theme fit for a supermarket in Amsterdam or Italy. Tara and I talked to the bartender, Adam, who is rated one of the best in the world. After letting him know about my tequila preference, he made me an El Camino: mezcal, sherry, tropical fruit, and spice. It was delicious and provided a great compliment to our four-course meal ahead. Our energetic and kind waiter, part-time cinematographer, and part-time fine-dining server gave us a rundown of the menu, divided into sections similar to my book: appetizers, midcourse, entrées.

Everywhere I go, I always ask one fundamental question which can be iterated in many ways: "What is the most popular dish?" or "What does the chef recommend tonight?" or "What are you known for?" After discussion, we settled on Hamachi Crudo, tempura-fried maitake, black truffle gnocchi, Japanese sweet potato agnolotti, and poached ora king salmon. When speaking with the talented Sous Chef, he discussed working with a private supplier providing the salmon. Tara, who has worked in the supplier business for years, described this process as the lovely platters and servers presented each dish. The dining experience was filmed on iPhone and will be condensed and potentially delivered to some connections at Fox.

When asking Camino about his goals this year, his response was very purposeful and intentional: "I want to earn a Michelin star." The chef's name is included with Daniel Humm and Drew Nieporent because of his ambition. Like Van Atta of Wine Cellar and Dino Tekdemir of Anatolian Kitchen, Camino gives it up to his all-star staff, who are enthusiastic and driven every day. It is a testament to Camino's down-to-earth, no BS nature, which bleeds through to his authentic team. His humility and refined character play well into the restaurant's upscale and celebratory vibe.

While Tara and I were filming there, we met Leiti Hsu, or "The Dining Dominatrix," self-proclaimed. A first-generation fine-dining regular, Hsu is well connected in the restaurant community and regularly hosts dinners with her friends. Hsu and I are having more sit-down dinners to discuss potential partnerships in the future with restaurants and chefs.

EXCLUSIVE DINING EXPERIENCE: MELROSE CAL-ITALIAN RESTAURANT, SPARTINA LOS ANGELES (TARA ELAINE BRENNAN, STEPHEN KALT, AND ME)

On March 1, 2022, I finished my one class from 12 p.m. to 1:50 p.m. for the day called Strategic Management and ran a Moneythink mentoring session with my high schoolers in the afternoon. Esteemed chef Stephen Kalt was preparing for Tara Brennen and me to arrive for an early dinner at his Spartina concept located on Melrose Avenue. I was in my classic blue suit with a striped blue and green button-down, and Tara was in her green overalls and her camo hat. Chef Kalt, Tara, and I enjoyed a long dinner on the patio that Chef Kalt exclaims, transports his customers, and makes them feel comfortable.

Out of Kalt's unusually long menu, he ordered for us some of his favorites: Grilled Avocado, Neapolitan Meatballs, Garlic Spaghettini, Short Rib Tortellini, Diver Scallops, Baja Shrimp and Prince Edward Island Mussels. Kalt, considered one of the "OG's" in the business and a Food Network guest, gave us an exclusive tour of his busy kitchen. He also told me about the secrets behind his success: his French cooking training and being fortunate to find such a great spot in Los Angeles that features an expansive patio. I will be keeping in touch with Kalt as he plans to open a Spartina By the Beach and follow through on more creative endeavors in his life inspired by his documentarian wife and son, who will be attending the University of Chicago.

ONE OF THE BEST INDIAN RESTAURANTS BUILT AND SOLD BY A FELLOW USC STUDENT

It was 11 a.m. on Thursday, February 10. I was chatting with football player, entrepreneur, and model Adrienne Smith, who was visiting USC for the day. I then overheard the man behind me discuss how he created and sold an Indian restaurant in Pune. I was intrigued because of my love for Indian food, so I turned around and introduced myself to Abhishek Pasricha, who was with a commander who served in the Indian Army for twenty-two years. I met with Abhi twice in February of 2022 to discuss his story.

Abhishek Pasricha is a USC MBA IBEAR with more than ten years of experience. His program at USC features sixteen nationalities and fifty-five people. The average years of experience for the program is around fourteen to twenty-five years. Abhi will graduate in June after completing the one-year MBA program for people already in their respective careers professionally.

He has worked at IBM for eight and half years, Deloitte for two years, and then EY for three months before coming to USC. He has worked in telecom, automotive technology, and oil and gas. From 2015 to 2017, he managed a restaurant in Pune, India serving 2,000 plus unique customers. His restaurant was one of the most successful in the city because of the location near the airport, top companies, and Symbiosis University in Pune.

Like me, Abhi has been a foodie throughout his life, and when he was with IBM, he used to travel a lot because he had clients all over the world. He has traveled across various spots of India, and he used to try several different kinds of cuisines. He connected with bloggers and foodies. He started getting invites to restaurant openings, so he could review them. Similar to how I am treated with my friend Tara, Abhi has been invited to restaurants to test new food. He was part of the Food Bloggers Association of India and PEO (Pune Eat Out) group. He would always spare one day to explore the food and cuisine of that city. Like me, one of his favorite activities is to try new restaurants. One example was when he went to an island in Indonesia and experienced Kopi Luwak, one of the most expensive coffees in the world. The most popular dish was N2S Fusion Meal (Fusion of North and South India in one meal) consisting of wood-baked Amritsari Kulcha (Stuffed Bread) with oil-free curry and Dosa (Indian Crepe).

He met his cofounder through his religion. He visited the Temple every Thursday in Pune, and he met a man with the same passion named Prabhakar. From there, after three or four months of discussion and planning, they came up with their own company and brand called North2South of JSK Bliss Foods LLP.

He decided to use a rolling pin as a design concept. He wanted to use 100,000 rolling pins on the ceiling of his restaurant. He installed 200 rolling pins in the ceiling of his restaurant. He also utilized it in the logo.

He wanted to have a competitive location allowing him to serve many people in the most efficient way possible. He finalized one location in Viman Nagar in Pune, an area with over 410 restaurants. He knew there was a lot of competition, and he knew if he succeeded in this area, he could do anything. He instilled an undaunted attitude. However, he lost a lot of money when he was searching for a place in 104°F weather. He had to bike because a car was never feasible. That original location also had unfortunate circumstances that presented too much risk to utilize. So, he found another location in Viman Nagar and renovated it himself.

Commitment while Working on the Side

- He could not be there on the first day opening because he had to travel for his other work at a large multinational company.
- 8:00 a.m. to 6:00 p.m. at consulting office.
- 6:00 p.m. to 1:00 a.m. at North2South.

Handling Operations

- Sixteen employees and a manager who managed the whole restaurant.
- Never had experience to handle so many employees, so he used his technology consulting experience to manage it in an efficient way.
- On his own, he made software and tools to understand how much ingredients he needed so he could manage food waste, storage, and inventory.
- He automated as many processes as he could, so he could see if there was any problem or spoilage going on.
- He had to act as lawyer, HR, salesman, and hired a part-time accountant.

Sales Increase Strategies

- QR Code every day new offers.
- Every Month new offering for one cent.
- Tie up with Tourism Industry (partnering with Uber and buses).
- Tie up with Colleges.
- Tie up with the corporate.

Restaurant Kitchen Caught Fire

- One day, one of the chefs forgot to lower the flame and the ceiling of the restaurant kitchen caught fire.
- Staff was preparing food and suddenly he got a call that there was a fire at his restaurant and his heart sank because he treated his employees as his family members.
- He reached the place forty minutes and saw four fire brigades standing outside of restaurant, but they controlled the fire after thirty-five minutes of watering his restaurant.
- No one was hurt, but he had to redo the whole kitchen.
- Employees then became demotivated, but he motivated them that they were safe.
- Took his twelve days to renovate the whole setup again and restart the restart.

Founders Conflicts

- His restaurant was starting to have a long wait time because there was a capacity of forty to fifty people.
- Big shopping center nearby and there were a lot of people centralized there.

- His cofounder did not agree with his ambition to have one hundred plus restaurants in all of India and expand afterward (North and south fusion restaurants, traveled to Northern and Southern parts of India to create a fusion).

- Shopping center invited him to expand, but there were difficulties when his partner was handling partners (his partner always had a negative attitude).

- Food spoilage was a lot, and there was an irregularity in the accounting.

- Entered several conflicts and looked for investors, and finally sold it for about 54,000 dollars to RAPSCO Industries owner.

BEST BÁNH MÍS IN LOS ANGELES

On Saturday, October 2, 2021, Tommy Nguyen and I went on a Warren Bennis Scholar retreat in Long Beach, California. We did a ropes course during the retreat, testing our limits emotionally and physically. Afterward, we were excited to try Tommy's family restaurant, known for serving the best Vietnamese Báhn Mí sandwiches in Los Angeles, Bánh Mi Saigon 168.

Tommy's father, Hong Nguyen, first started baking bread after taking refuge in a bakery while on the run for deserting the Vietnamese military during the Vietnam Cambodian War. His bread-making story started after the Fall of Saigon. After Tommy's grandfather's imprisonment in a reeducation camp, his father found himself forced to find work at eighteen and end his dream of studying abroad.

His father, unable to find any traditional work, began working as a smuggler. His job would require transporting goods like gasoline, coal, wood, and flour on trains for the underground market.

When the Vietnam Cambodian War began, the country implemented a national draft, and Nguyen decided to be the drafted representative of the family. While in a holding camp where drafted soldiers received reeducation, he realized the suicidal path of remaining in the army. On the way to Cambodia, Nguyen's military convoy stopped at one of the towns he used to smuggle goods in. At night, he silently slipped away and began a life on the run. He lived house to house, trying to survive using his old contacts and posts from his smuggling days.

After a couple of years, Nguyen took refuge in a bakery, where he smuggled flour. Every day, he would wake up to the smell of pastries and baguettes. He fell in love with the craft, and the baker began to train his father in the art of bread-making. Nguyen would soon become an expert in making bread and opened a small corner bánh mí stand, eventually opening his bakery. However, during this time, Nguyen was still on the run and had no official citizenship documents with the new Vietnamese government. This situation meant he could receive punishment for treason during the nightly curfews and random police identification inspections across Vietnam.

He lived in a paranoid state for years because of this. Ironically, his bakery became a popular place for the local police in the district. He was terrified of them but responded to their constant presence with kindness and gratitude. He would give them free coffee and bánh mís, and eventually become good friends. After a night out with the group of police officers, Nguyen finally confessed he deserted years ago during the war and had no identification. He asked his now good friends if they could help. Three days later, the police officers gifted Nguyen with a new citizenship ID, and he finally became a citizen of his own country again.

Fast forward to the early 1990s, he had the opportunity to immigrate to the United States because of his grandfather's time in a reeducation camp. Nguyen immigrated to the United States in 1994 with his father and brothers. He looked for jobs as a janitor and baker but could not find an opportunity for work. Eventually, he would find work as a waiter at a Chinese Seafood Restaurant and as a newspaper boy. Through a very frugal lifestyle and a saving effort between Nguyen and his brothers, they were able to open their first bánh mí shop in 1996.

The business was rough at first. There were few customers, and my aunts would cry most days in fear of the store closing. My father would also spend most nights sleeping in the bakery by the oven to wake up early to make the dough. But the legend of our bread and bánh mí sandwiches started to grow. We began to have loyal customers, who were refugees themselves. And as a community, we began to survive and thrive. Hong Nguyen and his brothers have opened over eight bakeries across California. They have recognition by the *Los Angeles Times* and other food circles for our authentic bánh mís and no fuss service. It may just be a delicious Vietnamese sandwich, but this bánh mí has given my friend's father and his family a new start in life.

THE YELP ELITE: AN INTERVIEW WITH TIFFANY ARDRON

Tiffany Ardron, the wife of one of the many role models in my life, Jacob Ardron, has quickly impressed me with the quick and easy reviews she performs when we have lunch every Sunday. Whenever I run into Tiffany, a native New Yorker, I usually hear a new story about the perks she receives due to her commitment to the crowd-sourced review application called Yelp. Unless you live under a rock, you've probably heard of the review site Yelp. Maybe you've recognized that red sticker on the window before entering a location that participates with Yelp. Or perhaps you and a friend were contemplating where to eat, and someone suggested pulling up some reviews or pictures on their app.

It's hard to be a foodie anywhere and not come across this helpful review and rating site. However, fewer people may have heard of Y.E.S or Yelp Elite Squad. Yelp Elite is a yearly program that recognizes the individuals in the community active in sharing the content of businesses on their platform. This content comes in the forms of eloquently detailed business reviews, tips, photos, check-ins, answering questions of curious community members, and other helpful content. Tiffany Ardron has been a member of Yelp Elite since 2019. Not only does the review site recognize Elite Squad members with a colorful badge on their profiles, but they also invite them to exclusive events, restaurant tastings, and many other perks.

Being from New York, Ardron always appreciated the diversity and details of food. You could count on her to share with her close friends a new restaurant or coffee shop she visited along with her favorite thing she ordered. You may have even gotten a slideshow of photos on her phone from the interior design or plate she called to her dessert! She used to share everything she now posts on Yelp just by word of mouth. Then when she started using Yelp more intentionally, she could now share more foodie decisions and photos with a larger community.

Her favorite part of using the app is getting connected to a business she would have never thought to try out. For example, during Black History Month or Asian American Pacific Islander Month, she made it a goal to visit a different Black-owned business or AAPI owned business for that entire month. She found businesses that were woman-run. If it weren't for this platform, she might not have had the exposure to such beautiful and creative businesses in my area!

Because of the pandemic, many of her favorite restaurants found it difficult to stay open due to closing down their indoor dining. She firmly believes that every restaurant deserves a five-star review for working hard to remain open. However, she still has many recommendations in her review of the food, parking, staff, and overall location details that she would want to know. But everywhere she went, she gave five-star reviews. Her parents raised her to always appreciate people who serve you, from our mailman to our waiter to the grocery store helper. This conviction has over flowed to the things I post on Yelp.

For the three years, she has been a Yelp Elite member, I have been able to experience even more opportunities within the community than the average person on Yelp. She received invitations to private events at restaurants or museums. Other times, local businesses rebranding or opening a new location want to spread the word! That's where active Yelp users within the Yelp Elite community come in. She did not start reviewing businesses in the hopes of becoming part of the Elite Squad. After sharing posts on Yelp for some time, the elite manager reached out to her on the app, inviting her to join this community. She has loved it ever since!

If anything, this badge inspires her to visit new places and post even more. And she tries to get her friends and family to use the app more to enjoy some of the perks she's experienced on Yelp Elite, such as menu tastings and events. In addition, Y.E.S. has allowed her to explore even more parts of her city and connect with even more amazing businesses than she would have on her own.

OMICRON CONTINUES?

According to a 2021 article posted by AP News by Don Thompson, because of COVID-19, it will take California a few years to open back up completely, as about a third of the restaurants permanently closed while two-thirds of workers lost their jobs. However, the industry will rebound soon, hopefully producing 160,000 jobs by 2029 for two million statewide. As of 2022, most restaurants in my hometown that have reopened still require a face mask when a party walks in, but everyone is allowed to take the masks off once seated.

We will see if there will ever be a world where masks are not synonymous with the dining experience, but at the moment, that is not the case and may not ever be for a very long time, with the omicron variant spreading at the beginning of 2022, causing many universities, including my own, to resort to online classes for a week. Hopefully, we will handle this virus in a few years, and a maskless entrance into a five-star restaurant will be like walking down an award show red carpet.

POPULAR RESTAURANTS WELL-KNOWN IN THE UNITED STATES

ACCORDING TO THE 2021 *LOS ANGELES MAGAZINE* ARTICLE, "HOW CALIFORNIA-BORN RESTAURANTS CONQUERED AMERICA"

The Brown Derby, founded in 1926, became a hot spot for big names in Hollywood to visit. The classic restaurant was designed by set designers and financed by studio executives. It also helped that it was located across from one of the nicest hotels in Los Angeles at the time, The Ambassador. Actors, musicians, and Hollywood sweethearts could not resist the quality classic American food, specifically owner Bob Cobb's very own salad creation of lettuce, tomato, chicken, bacon, eggs, avocado, and Roquefort. This magnificent green combination became known as the Cobb salad, a mainstay on many American and International restaurant menus.

Glen Bell, a student at San Bernardino High School, took inspiration from McDonald's to create the Mexican food equivalent with his entrepreneurial mindset. In 1962, he opened Taco Bell in Downey, California, attempting to offer the best Mexican food with classic hard-shell tacos and the utmost efficiency. Bell was inspired by a Mexican restaurant near his house called Mitla Café, which was famous for its hard-shelled tacos. Bell opened a stand in 1951 with the name of Taco-Tia, then El Taco, to eventually Taco Bell. Today, the leading Mexican fast-food chain serves over two billion customers a year at more than 7,727 restaurants in thirty-one countries throughout the world.

Pancakes have long stood the test of time as a popular item on any quality breakfast menu. Filmmaker Al Lapin was riding around in Burbank by the studios when he saw that many Los Angelenos were lining up to get Bob's Big Boy. Across the street, there was a building open to rent. Lapin utilized his craving, borrowed some money, and opened up the first International House of Pancakes in 1958 in Toluca Lake, Los Angeles, California. Lapin founded the restaurant with Jeremy Lapin and Albert Kallis with the help of Sherwood Rosenberg and William Kaye. With crazy recipes like the Tahitian Orange Pineapple pancakes, the spot became popular and started to expand. In 1973, they shortened the chain's name to "IHOP" for marketing purposes. Today, the company has 1,841 restaurants in the Americas, the Middle East, and the Indian subcontinent.

In 1922, Lawrence L. "Lawry" Frank and Walter Van de Kamp founded the Lawry's Company and created the self-proclaimed oldest restaurant in Los Angeles called Tam O'Shanter Inn in Atwater Village. In 1938, the two businessmen and steak lovers opened Lawry's The Prime Rib on La Cienega Boulevard in Beverly Hills. The classic restaurant, which served one entrée for the longest time, standing rib roast, was the cornerstone of Restaurant Row in Beverly Hills. The pair's love of food and global food imprint spans well before the creation of their empire. Frank and Kamp produced generations of snacks at their Glassell Park Plant such as their famous homemade potato chips that have undoubtedly inspired many chip manufacturers today. At their California test kitchen, the families created seasoning salt and spices and still have a line of fish sticks that can most likely be found in the freezer aisle of your nearby grocery store.

John Galardi, the new high school graduate, was just having fun and trying to make money when he took a job at Taco

Bell. He worked part-time for fifty cents an hour at Taco-Tia. Gallardi rose through the ranks at Taco Bell, essentially becoming a manager. An opportunity of a lifetime came to Gallardi when he was presented the chance to lease an open restaurant in Wilmington and create his own brand. Bell, his former boss, stressed that it could not be Mexican food. Gallardi decided on hot dogs and his wife helped him come up with the interesting name while looking through a cookbook: Wienershnitzel. The store, which is still recognizable by its signature A-style roofs, is now considered the World's Largest Hot Dog Chain, serving many states in the US, Panama, and Guam.

After World War II, the Los Angeles farmland was rapidly transformed into a suburban city with freeways and infrastructure. Harry and Esther Snyder relocated to Baldwin Park from Seattle in 1948. To finance their home, the Snyders opened a hamburger stand near their house that became the first-ever hamburger drive-thru stand in California. Before then, carhops used to serve customers in their cars. Harry created a two-way speaker and Esther handled the accounting side of the business. Because of the efficiency, the Snyders called their family restaurant In-N-Out. Today, the In-N-Out restaurant chain has maintained a loyal customer base while expanding slowly to the rest of California and other western US states while remaining private to optimize customer satisfaction.

Dave Burham made a living serving hot dogs and lemonade to strong people in Muscle Beach next to the Santa Monica Pier in Los Angeles, California. Burham originally called his store Party Puffs but changed it to the more fitting Hot Dog on a Stick. Today, one can see the classic restaurant at an indoor mall outlet or at the Los Angeles County Fair, where there are usually eight set up. Today, there are also internationally franchised locations in Korea and Shanghai, China.

Life is not complete without dessert. Burt Baskin owned Burt's Ice Cream while Irv Robbins operated Snowbird Ice Cream in Glendale. After Baskin married Robbins' sister, the two brothers-in-law came together to create the largest frozen-dessert shops on the planet in 1948. They called their ice cream parlor Baskin-Robbins and served a whopping 31 flavors. By 1948, the pair were already operating six stores in Southern California with the original one located in Glendale. Today, the iconic brand has almost 2,500 shops in the United States and 5,000 shops in nearly fifty countries worldwide.

INTRODUCTION OF CREDIT CARDS

Credit cards were a massive addition to the restaurant scene. Before they existed, restaurants like Le Pavillon provided house accounts for their favorite customers. According to a 2013 blog post on *Restaurant-ing Through History* called "Charge-It," the credit card was invented on February 8, 1950, when returned to Major's Cabin Grill in New York City with a Diners Club Card. He made the first ever charge in history on a nationwide credit card with just a pen and paper. When credit cards became popular in the 1950s, many restaurants refused to accept them. American Express went as far as to finance restaurants because they were scared restaurants would never use their card.

STANFORD EXPERIENCE EXPLAINED

Steve Blank, successful founder of many start-ups and entrepreneurship professor at Stanford and University of California Berkeley Haas School of Business, launched a famous "Lean Launchpad" class. Blank created the iterative customer development program that fed into the revolutionary lean start-up movement, a fair designation given to start-ups defining them as different organizations than larger corporations and therefore requiring their own set of processes to flourish.

Blank created a class called Hacking for Defense which has since been adopted by the US Department of Defense. During the pandemic, he pivoted this class to be called Hacking4Recovery, a week-long class where companies could present to Stanford professors and Silicon Valley VCs interested in investing in early-stage start-ups.

PHONE CALLS

I called Delilah, a spot I love in West Hollywood, on the day after Doja Cat's birthday party to an exhausted voice on the phone. I was looking to partner with them, either a book contribution or hosting a party. Unfortunately, I never followed up due to my finals schedule of twenty-one units and handling my nonprofit back at home. I look forward to doing a launch party in the summer there.

Joy Limanon, the Founder and Principal at Peridot, was a pleasure to work with. I made an urgent call to her early on Super Bowl Sunday, and she picked up, and we discussed partnerships for about ten minutes. I had just eaten at Felix Trattoria and enjoyed their incredible Pizze Margherita and Focaccia Romana Rosa. Evan Funke, culinary storyteller and one of the best pasta makers in the world, received word of my book, and I was discussing with Joy the possibilities for the busy man to contribute. His podcast with Joe Rogan on the art of making pasta is fantastic.

Former CEO and cofounder of one of the top start-up beverage companies in the United States wrote an impactful potential foreword for my book, but the partnership did not pan out. I was thinking of doing a cover based on Norman Rockwell's turkey feast painting, and when I let her know, there was a slight disagreement, so we parted ways, unfortunately. It was a great discussion between fellow entrepreneurs.

ACKNOWLEDGMENTS

This book would not have been possible without the love and support of the many people I am lucky to call family and friends. To you, I am forever grateful.

I must start with my education at Archbishop Mitty High School, California Polytechnic State University–San Luis Obispo, the University of Southern California, and Stanford University. These institutions have provided me with the insights to analyze my life in a special way and continuously grow throughout my life.

A huge thank you to Tara Elaine Brennan for her contribution to the forward and her guidance and grace during the last few months before my publication. Our synergy made crossing the finish line efficient.

Thank you to my mentors Varun Soni and David Belasco for taking an interest in my story and contributing to the book's foreword. Thank you to Philip Camino of Fellow and Imari and Stephen Kalt of Spartina for hosting me and Tara, as well as filming collaborative TV content. Thank you to Michael Mina for trusting a college student and believing in me.

Thank you to the staff at Craig's for always seating my friends and me when we showed up on Tuesday nights. I must also thank the staff at Café Mak and Bird's Nest Café, two places I frequently visited during the fall of 2021 and the spring of 2022. Finally, I want to express gratitude to the PR team and the owners of The London West Hollywood, Craig's, Bird's Nest, Bestia, Bavel, Delilah, Pink Taco, Café Mak, Elephante, Felix Trattoria, Urth Caffé, Yamashiro Hollywood, and Redbird.

Thank you to my Aunt Suz, Uncle Bill, and my cousins Erik and Erin for letting me stay at their houses in Nipomo every time I got stuck on my trek between Northern California and Southern California.

I need to thank God, my close-knit family, and best friends from my hometown in Los Gatos, Glendale, and South Central for giving me the time and emotional support I needed to relive some fantastic experiences and tell my story.

Thank you to my mom and dad, Jeanette and Gregg Rasmussen, and my brother, Luke Rasmussen, for their lifelong unconditional love and support, and specifically for supporting me in my erratic professional career as I finished up my undergraduate academic career at the University of Southern California.

I must also thank the many individuals who helped me through some turbulent moments in my life over the past year and provided me with many unforgettable times. Those people include Jacob Ardron, Tiffany Ardron, Jose Rodriguez, Lorena Rodriguez, Chris Rodriguez, Daphne Mall, Juvensen Jules, Daniel Lua, Greg Russell, Brannon Rowan, Caleb Bermudez, Anthony Chang, Angel Muñoz, Ralph Lua, Daniel Lua, Kyle Kan, Stephanie Souza, Kayla

Dawis, Gema Martínez, Claudia Mejía, Kyla Jones, Natalie Dean, Camille Dean, Charlotte Knapp, Greg Knapp, Quinton Markett, Parth Mehta, Evan Vemury, Ashlyn Plant, Abby Allen, Brady Allen, Bryan Kim, Harry Vaughan Williams, Isabella Acunto, Sophia Acunto, Paul D'Angelo, Jared Gee, Nick Imig, Helena Ordin, Olivia Frary, Marina Eliopoulos, Max Reed, Ryan Lee, Mackenzie Boatman, Natalia Parraz, Tommy Nguyen, Zazu Lippert, John Medlinskas, Matthew Bui, Seun Omonije, Jerry Bao, Josiah Norwood, Jacarti Emiliano De Contreras, Ariana Papadopoulos, Sydney Zima, Drew Quall, Matthew Clement, Max Coulson, Mateo Pastrana, Will Fox, Ariana Martino, Katharine Foster, Rachel Lindsay, and so many more.

Thank you to all the people who accompanied me on my 2021 trips across California and to Las Vegas, Puerto Vallarta, Chicago, New York, and New Jersey. Rest in peace to Greg Knapp, who texted me regularly during my Wells Fargo internship and while I wrote this book. He lent me his Cadillac Escalade and let me stay at his Summit, New Jersey townhouse, during the summer, opening his fridge to me and texting me restaurant recommendations every day.

Thank you to all the groups I am a part of that have given me a strong community and allowed me to always go after my dreams, including Tau Kappa Epsilon, my Warren Bennis Scholar cohort, Moneythink USC, Shaukat Initiative, USC Undergraduate Student Government, Scholars of Finance, Screen360tv, the Stanford Summer Session community, the USC Entrepreneurship Forum group, the BoohooMAN model community, Marshall Student Ambassadors, the Glendale City Church community, Craig's community, and all other groups I have been in.

I must thank the team at New Degree Press for their hard work in supporting me on my publishing journey, including David Grandouiller, Brian Bies, Leila Summers, Stacey Hickman, Anne Belott, Carter Woetzel, Michelle Pollack, Christy Mossburg, and John Saunders. I also need to thank Eric Koester of the Creator Institute and Georgetown University for his encouragement and coaching.

I also spoke to several individuals while writing this book, many of whom shared direct and candid insights about their entrepreneurial journeys and restaurant concepts. Thank you to Julie Van Atta, the Kims, Dino Tekdemir, Dave Perlick, TJ Callahan, Ori Menashe, Genevieve Gergis, Daniel Humm, Alice Waters, Wolfgang Puck, Jeremiah Tower, Gabriel Stulman, Ann Kim, Christina Nguyen, Jamie Malone, and all the inspiring owners and chefs featured in this book.

Thank you to the teachers of my spring 2022 semester at the University of Southern California (my last semester of my undergraduate career): Christopher Herrar, David Belasco, Francis Pereira, Joe Raffiee, Daniel Fehder, Shelley Smith, Jeffrey Fellenzer, Joe Saltzman, and Varun Soni.

Finally, I also want to thank the very generous group of individuals who purchased a copy of this book during the presale. You are the ones that made the publication of this story possible. Thank you for investing in my story and my writing. This group includes:

Aaron Reed	Alexis Areias
Abby Allen	Amir Behbahani
Abby Norman	Arturo Barajas
Aditya Sudini	Ashley Chhabra
Alana T Karen	Berit Marcum

Beth and Tony Lama

Betsy Toomey

Brandon White

Brannon Rowan

Brian Lundquist

Brian Yuen

Bryan Kim

Caleb Bermudez

Cameron Lahitette

Catherine Kavanaugh

Cathy Norman

Charlotte Knapp

Chris Lim

Christina Aitchison

Chynna Hinrichsen

Craig Jerman

Craig Seidel

Curtis J Barcal

Daniel Lua

Daphne Mall

David Bohline

Dino Tekdemir

Donald DuBrow

Dr. Ginny Baro

Elena Carter

Elzbieta Najlis

Eric Koester

Evan Vemury

Gema Martinez

Judy Grosey

Gregg T Rasmussen

Heather Knox

Heidi Redmond

Helena Ordin

Isaac Huezo

Izayah Powell

Jack Saperstone

Jaclene Nunes

Jacob Ardron

Jai Bansal

James Baker

James McFarlane

James Roake

James Weslow

Janean Plant

Jared Gee

Jeanette Rasmussen

Jennifer Aguirre

Jerry Bao

Joanne Lewis

John Medlinskas

John Worden

John and Teri Grosey

Jon Rasmussen

Jordan Sins

Jordan Trief

Joseph S Joseph

Josephine Cheung

Joshua Fakhri

Olivia Frary

Juvensen Jules
Kate Le Blanc
Katherine Wesmiller
Kathy and Kent Goodin
Kelly Shannon
Kevin Kaauwai
Kris Bubic
Kristen Kelly
Lisa Starr
Luke Rasmussen
Lynn Buckley
Mallika Samtani
Marco Torres
Martin Park
Mary Frances Lynch
Matthew Bui
Nadine Paulsen
Natalia Parraz
Nickey Knighton
Nicole Napiltonia
Nike Taylor
Nina Lamour

Patti Foley
Philip Dapaah
Rayana Ramirez
Rroki Marvukaj
Ryan Lee
Seun Omonije
Shannon Splaine
Shelley Hopkins
Simon Park
Sodabeh Fazlollahi
Stacey Dougherty
Stephanie Blanchard
Summer Short
Tamara Black
Tara Elaine Brennan
Vanessa Chen
Vicky Fowler
Vlad Haukelid
William Rasmussen
Yvette Marchand
Yvette Markett

As well as others who chose to remain anonymous.

APPENDIX

INTRODUCTION

Bellini, Jarrett. "The No. 1 Thing to Consider before Opening a Restaurant." *CNBC*, July 6, 2016. https://www.cnbc.com/2016/01/20/heres-the-real-reason-why-most-restaurants-fail.html.

Center for Biological Diversity. "Food Waste Is Trashing the Planet." *Take Extinction Off Your Plate*, 2019. https://www.biologicaldiversity.org/takeextinctionoffyourplate/waste/index.html.

FSR. "Report: Restaurant Sales to Top $1.2 Trillion by 2030." *FSR Magazine*, November 5, 2019. https://www.fsrmagazine.com/content/report-restaurant-sales-top-12-trillion-2030.

Guest Opinion. "Coronavirus Will Have Lasting Impact on Restaurant Industry." *Food Safety News*, April 8, 2021. https://www.foodsafetynews.com/2021/02/coronavirus-will-have-lasting-impact-on-restaurant-industry/.

Noguchi, Yuki. "16 States Now Have Obesity Rates 35% or Higher. That's 4 More States than Last Year."

Health. NPR, September 21, 2021. https://www.npr.
org/2021/09/21/1039393839/16-states-now-have-obesity-rates-
35-or-higher-thats-4-more-states-than-last-year.

Ozimek, Adam. "No, Most Restaurants Don't Fail in the First
Year." *Forbes*, February 3, 2017. https://www.forbes.com/sites/
modeledbehavior/2017/01/29/no-most-restaurants-dont-fail-
in-the-first-year/?sh=688bea444fcc.

CHAPTER 1: BIRTH OF HISTORICAL CALIFORNIA RESTAURANT SCENE

Blank, Steve. "Steve Blank the Lean Launchpad Class: It's the
Same, but Different." *Steve Blank*, June 16, 2021. https://
steveblank.com/2019/03/26/the-lean-launchpad-class-its-the-
same-but-different/.

Bloch, Sam. "To Survive the Pandemic, Restaurants Are
Offering Subscriptions for Bottomless Coffee and Beer. Will
the Model Last?" *The Counter*, November 7, 2020. https://
thecounter.org/restaurant-subscriptions-coffee-beer-covid-
19-pandemic-panera/.

Bradesca, Kathryne. "The History of California Cuisine &
Home Cooking." *Munchery*, September 7, 2020. https://www.
munchery.com/blog/history-of-california-cuisine-and-
home-cooking/.

Canvas.index "Strategy & Innovation." *Lumos Business*. http://
lumosbusiness.com/tag/canvas-index/.

Cision PR Newswire. "National Restaurant Association
Releases 2021 State Of The Restaurant Industry Report."
National Restaurant Association, January 26, 2021. https://
www.prnewswire.com/news-releases/national-restaurant-

association-releases-2021-state-of-the-restaurant-industry-report-301214592.html.

Feldman, Eli. "Minimum Viable Restaurants." *Medium*, January 20, 2015. https://medium.com/@EliFeldman/minimum-viable-restaurants-2da356344892.

Osterwalder, Alex. "I'm Alex Osterwalder." *About Alex*, 2021. https://www.alexosterwalder.com/.

Ries, Eric. 2019. *The Lean Startup: How Constant Innovation Creates Radically Successful Businesses*. New York: Crown Publishing Group.

Ries, Eric. 2017. *The Startup Way: How Modern Companies Use Entrepreneurial Management to Transform Culture and Drive Long-Term Growth*. New York: Currency.

Romeo, Peter, and Myra Engers Weinberg. "Timeline: How Today's Restaurant Industry Came to Be." *Restaurant Business*, March 25, 2019. https://www.restaurantbusinessonline.com/special-reports/timeline-how-todays-restaurant-industry-came-be.

Romeo, Peter. "Restaurant Sales to Jump 10.2% in 2021, National Restaurant Association Says." *Restaurant Business*, January 26, 2021. https://www.restaurantbusinessonline.com/financing/restaurant-sales-jump-102-2021-national-restaurant-association-says.

Roos, Dave. "When Did People Start Eating in Restaurants?" History.com, May 18, 2020. https://www.history.com/news/first-restaurants-china-france.

Simkin, John. "Immigration to the USA: 1900–1920." Spartacus Educational, January 2020. https://spartacus-educational. com/USAE1900.htm.

The Food Timeline. "Traditional State Foods & Recipes." The Food Timeline History Notes-State Foods, January 30, 2015. https://www.foodtimeline.org/statefoods.html#calmissions.

Wiener-Bronner, Danielle. "Restaurants Are Transforming into Grocery Stores Because of Coronavirus." *CNN Business.* CNN, April 8, 2020. https://www.cnn.com/2020/04/08/ business/restaurants-grocery-stores-coronavirus/index.html.

CHAPTER 2: INCORPORATE A BUSINESS MODEL CANVAS ASAP

Encyclopædia Britannica Online. s.v. "McDonald's." Accessed March 3, 2022. https://www.britannica.com/topic/ McDonalds.

Mazurek, Brie. "Inside the California Food Revolution." *CUESA,* January 6, 2016. https://cuesa.org/article/inside-california-food-revolution.

Nichols, Chris. "How California-Born Restaurants Conquered America." *Los Angeles Magazine,* July 23, 2021. https://www. lamag.com/digestblog/california-born-restaurants/.

NSTATE, LLC. "California Economy." *Economy,* December 2017. https://www.netstate.com/economy/ca_economy.htm.

Oldest.org. "8 Oldest Restaurants in California." *Food,* September 5, 2019. https://www.oldest.org/food/restaurants-in-california/.

Quebec, Alexander. "10 Restaurant Chains That Got Their Start in California." *RSS*, January 12, 2016. https://caliplate.com/10-restaurant-chains-that-got-their-start-in-california/.

Romeo, Peter, and Myra Engers Weinberg. "Timeline: How Today's Restaurant Industry Came to Be." *Restaurant Business*, March 25, 2019. https://www.restaurantbusinessonline.com/special-reports/timeline-how-todays-restaurant-industry-came-be.

Roos, Dave. "When Did People Start Eating in Restaurants?" *History.com*, May 18 2020. https://www.history.com/news/first-restaurants-china-france.

The Food Timeline. "USA Food History." January 30, 2015. https://www.foodtimeline.org/usa.html.

Wimpsett, Emily. "Pop-up Restaurants: Everything You Need to Know." *QSR Automations*, January 26, 2021, https://www.qsrautomations.com/blog/restaurant-management/pop-up-restaurants/.

CHAPTER 3: HISTORY OF LARGE CHANGES IN THE INDUSTRY

Burton, Monica. "Two Years into #MeToo, Has Anything Really Changed?" *Eater*, December 5, 2019. https://www.eater.com/2019/12/5/20974733/metoo-restaurant-industry-recap-2019.

Caplan, Jeremy. "Restaurants Face Lean Times in the Economic Downturn." *Time*, October 10, 2008. http://content.time.com/time/nation/article/0,8599,1848402,00.html.

Ehler, James T. "Antoine Beauvilliers." *Who's Who: Antoine Beauvilliers*, March 3, 2022. http://www.foodreference.com/html/wantoinebeauvilliers.html.

Franck, Tom W. "Home Food Delivery Is Surging Thanks to Ease of Online Ordering, New Study Shows." *CNBC*, July 12, 2017. https://www.cnbc.com/2017/07/12/home-food-delivery-is-surging-thanks-to-ease-of-online-ordering-new-study-shows.html.

Gramlich, John. "10 Facts about Americans and Facebook." Pew Research Center, June 2, 2021. https://www.pewresearch.org/fact-tank/2021/06/01/facts-about-americans-and-facebook/.

Lehman Jr., Don. "The History of Fine Dining: Modern." Accessed January 1, 2022. http://donlehmanjr.com/Restaurant/Dining%20History/hfd3.htm.

Mealey, Lorri. "The Rise and Fall of the Restaurant Franchise." *The Balance Small Business*, March 26, 2019. https://www.thebalancesmb.com/history-of-restaurants-part-3-2888657.

Migliori, Simone. "How the Food Network Went from Bust to Big Time." *GBH*, July 23, 2018. https://www.wgbh.org/news/lifestyle/2018/07/23/how-the-food-network-went-from-bust-to-big-time.

Pew Research Center. "Public Views about Americans' Eating Habits." Science & Society, December 1, 2016. https://www.pewresearch.org/science/2016/12/01/public-views-about-americans-eating-habits/.

Romeo, Peter, and Myra Engers Weinberg. "Timeline: How Today's Restaurant Industry Came to Be." *Restaurant*

Business, Restaurant Business, March 25, 2019. https://www.
restaurantbusinessonline.com/special-reports/timeline-how-
todays-restaurant-industry-came-be.

SinglePlatform. "5 Ways America's Restaurant Industry
has Changed Over the Last Decade." TripAdvisor For
Restaurants, 2021. https://www.singleplatform.com/blog/
restaurant-industry/5-ways-americas-restaurant-industry-
has-changed-over-the-last-decade/.

Statista. "Total US Retail and Food Services Sales 2020." *Retail
& Trade.* Accessed February 17, 2022. https://www.statista.
com/statistics/197569/annual-retail-and-food-services-sales/.

Statista. "U.S.: Annual Unemployment Rate 1990–2018."
Economy. Accessed February 10, 2022. https://www.statista.
com/statistics/193290/unemployment-rate-in-the-usa-
since-1990/.

Sugar, Rachel. "How Food Network Turned Big-City Chef
Culture into Middle-America Pop Culture." *Grub Street,*
November 30, 2017. https://www.grubstreet.com/2017/11/
early-days-food-network-oral-history.html.

Thorn, Bret. "Pandemic Recovery Will Be Uneven, but
Restaurants Will Emerge Stronger, the NRA's Hudson
Riehle and BTIG's Peter Saleh Tell ICR Attendees." *Nation's
Restaurant News,* October 6, 2021. https://www.nrn.com/
operations/pandemic-recovery-will-be-uneven-restaurants-
will-emerge-stronger-nra-s-hudson-riehle-and.

Weinberger, Jerry. "America's Food Revolution." *City
Journal,* June 15, 2019. https://www.city-journal.org/html/
america%E2%80%99s-food-revolution-13217.html.

Whitaker, Jan. "Effects of World War I on Restaurant-Ing in the US." *World War I Centennial*, March 12, 2019. https://www.worldwar1centennial.org/index.php/communicate/press-media/wwi-centennial-news/6147-effects-of-world-war-i-on-restaurant-ing-in-us.html.

CHAPTER 4: FARM-TO-TABLE

Agran, Libby. "California Cuisine–Who Named It and When Did It Begin?" *Wine History Project of San Luis Obispo County*, August 10, 2019. https://winehistoryproject.org/california-cuisine-who-named-it-and-when-did-it-begin/.

Brunner, Rob. "5 Brilliant Business Lessons from Wolfgang Puck." *Fast Company*, November 21, 2017. https://www.fastcompany.com/3034674/5-brilliant-business-lessons-from-wolfgang-puck#:~:text=In%20the%20three%20decades%20since,express%20restaurants%20in%20the%20U.S.%2C.

Cimini, Marla. "California Culinary Revolution—Meet the Chef behind It." Travels with Marla, January 8, 2021. https://marlacimini.com/meet-the-chef-behind-the-california-culinary-revolution/.

Damewood, Andrea. "The Untold Story of Jeremiah Tower." *Portland Mercury*, May 31, 2017. https://www.portlandmercury.com/film/2017/05/31/19048578/the-untold-story-of-jeremiah-tower.

Encyclopædia Britannica Online. s.v. "Alice Waters." Accessed March 3, 2022. https://www.britannica.com/biography/Alice-Waters.

McSweeney, Margaret. "Chef Jeremiah Tower: A Shining Culinary Constellation." *Kitchen Chat*, July 23, 2021. https://

kitchenchat.info/chef-jeremiah-tower-a-shining-culinary-constellation/.

Rubin, Merle. "A Delicious Account of America's Culinary Revolution." *Los Angeles Times*, June 11, 2001. https://www.latimes.com/archives/la-xpm-2001-jun-11-cl-8961-story.html.

Star Chefs "Alice Waters' Biography." *Women & Food*, 2022. https://www.starchefs.com/features/women/html/bio_waters.shtml.

The Food Timeline. "American Presidents' Food Favorites." January 30, 2015. https://www.foodtimeline.org/presidents.html.

WolfgangPuck. "About—Wolfgang Puck." Accessed November 9, 2021. https://wolfgangpuck.com/about/.

CHAPTER 5: THE EVER-CHANGING AMERICAN DIET: PLANTS, PLANTS, AND MORE PLANTS

Avey, Tori. "From Pythagorean to Pescatarian–the Evolution of Vegetarianism." *PBS*, January 28, 2014. https://www.pbs.org/food/the-history-kitchen/evolution-vegetarianism/.

Chee, Chermaine. "Veganism Statistics in the US for 2022—How Many Vegans Are There in America?" *Truly Experiences Blog*, January 10, 2022. https://trulyexperiences.com/blog/veganism-statistics-usa/.

Greenwood, Chelsea. "Will Plant-Based Menus Take over the Restaurant Industry?" Shondaland, November 2, 2021. https://www.shondaland.com/act/a36766059/are-plant-based-menus-take-over-the-restaurant-industry/.

Gunnars, Kris. "5 Diets That Are Supported by Science."
Healthline, July 2, 2019. https://www.healthline.com/
nutrition/meal-plans.

J. Selby's. "A Plant Based Eatery." Accessed January 1, 2022.
https://www.jselbys.com/.

Kateman, Brian. "Vegan Restaurants Are on the Rise."
Forbes, August 21, 2019. https://www.forbes.com/sites/
briankateman/2019/08/21/vegan-restaurants-are-on-the-
rise/?sh=7650749b1e80.

Love Serve Remember. "Gracias Madre," 2021. https://www.
graciasmadre.co/.

Sentient Media. "Increase in Veganism: Why Is Veganism on
the Rise in 2021?" Sentient Media, October 26, 2021. https://
sentientmedia.org/increase-in-veganism/.

Šimčikas, Saulius, et al. "Is the Percentage of Vegetarians and
Vegans in the U.S. Increasing?" *Animal Charity Evaluators*,
September 26, 2020. https://animalcharityevaluators.org/
blog/is-the-percentage-of-vegetarians-and-vegans-in-the-u-
s-increasing/.

Starostinetskaya, Anna. "After Legal Battle, Vegan Restaurant by
Chloe Rebrands as Beatnic." *VegNews*, July 29, 2021. https://
vegnews.com/2021/7/by-chloe-rebrands-beatnic.

Suddath, Claire. "A Brief History of Veganism." *Time*, October
30, 2008. https://time.com/3958070/history-of-veganism/.

Vedge Restaurant "About—Vedge." *Vedge*, 2022. https://www.
vedgerestaurant.com/about/.

Watsky, David. "Best Vegetarian and Vegan Meal Delivery Services." *CNET*, February 17, 2022. https://www.cnet.com/health/nutrition/best-vegetarian-and-vegan-meal-delivery/.

CHAPTER 6: THE RISE OF WOMEN CHEFS

Biography.com Editors. "Julia Child Biography." Biography.com. Updated May 27, 2021. https://www.biography.com/personality/julia-child.

Culinary Depot Inc. "Five Famous Female Chefs and Their Stories." *Culinary Depot* (blog). Accessed November 8, 2020. https://www.culinarydepotinc.com/blog/five-famous-female-chefs-and-their-stories/.

Depler, Alicia. "American Women in World War Two: The Impact of Rationing and Shortages on Eating and Food Procurement." *New Errands: The Undergraduate Journal of American Studies* 4, no. 2 (Spring 2017). https://journals.psu.edu/ne/article/view/60343.

Greenwood, Chelsea. "The Triumph of Women Chefs." Shondaland, November 18, 2021. https://www.shondaland.com/live/travel-food/a35970320/the-triumph-of-women-chefs/.

LaGrave, Katherine. "Meet the Women behind Minneapolis's Food Revolution." *Vogue*, August 6, 2019. https://www.Vogue.com/article/women-minneapolis-food-revolution-james-beard.

Mbabazi, Donah. "Female Chef's Rise in the Culinary Industry." *The New Times | Rwanda*, November 12, 2020. https://www.newtimes.co.rw/lifestyle/female-chefs-rise-culinary-industry.

Sugar, Rachel. "How Food Network Turned Big-City Chef
Culture into Middle-America Pop Culture." *Grub Street*,
November 30, 2017. https://www.grubstreet.com/2017/11/
early-days-food-network-oral-history.html.

The Mob Museum. "Women's Rights Advanced During
Prohibition." *Prohibition*, https://prohibition.
themobmuseum.org/the-history/how-prohibition-changed-
american-culture/womens-rights/.

CHAPTER 7: PROMOTE POSITIVITY

Fenner, Justin. "How Gabriel Stulman Went from Making
Cheese Steaks to Running 6 NYC Restaurants." *GQ*, August
26, 2015. https://www.gq.com/story/gabriel-stulman-
interview.

Ozimek, Adam. "No, Most Restaurants Don't Fail in the First
Year." *Forbes*, February 3, 2017. https://www.forbes.com/sites/
modeledbehavior/2017/01/29/no-most-restaurants-dont-fail-
in-the-first-year/?sh=2c68dffa4fcc.

Seppälä, Emma, and Kim Cameron. "Proof That Positive Work
Cultures Are More Productive." *Harvard Business Review*,
May 8, 2017. https://hbr.org/2015/12/proof-that-positive-work-
cultures-are-more-productive.

Williams, Alex. "Gabriel Stulman, Restaurateur, and a Bit of
Wisconsin." *New York Times*, January 26, 2011. https://www.
nytimes.com/2011/01/27/fashion/27close.html.

CHAPTER 8: SERVICE MATTERS

Ockerbloom, Chrissy. "A Lesson from Gabriel Stulman on
Restaurant Turnover and Employee Engagement." *RockBot*

Blog, December, 2015. https://blog.rockbot.com/a-lesson-from-gabriel-stulman-on-restaurant-turnover-and-employee-engagement.

Spoon Mob. "Aaron Silverman." Accessed January 1, 2022. https://www.spoonmob.com/aaronsilverman.

TEDx Talks. "A Winning Recipe—Lessons from Restaurants on Engaging Your Team | Gabriel Stulman | TEDxCambridge." October 28, 2014. Video, 18:44. https://www.youtube.com/watch?v=sK-AW2ExST8.

Williams, Alex. "Gabriel Stulman, Restaurateur, and a Bit of Wisconsin." *New York Times*, January 26, 2011. https://www.nytimes.com/2011/01/27/fashion/27close.html.

CHAPTER 9: LOCATION CHANGES THE GAME: SPACE AND SAFETY

Mealey, Lorri. "Here Are Some Tips on Where You Should Locate Your Restaurant." *The Balance Small Business*, March 24, 2018. https://www.thebalancesmb.com/choosing-restaurant-location-2888543.

CHAPTER 10: EMBRACE ADVERSITY

Chaplin, Cathy. "Popular Taiwanese Breakfast Pop-up Eyes Permanent Roots in Chinatown." *Eater LA*, October 21, 2020. https://la.eater.com/2020/10/21/21524081/taiwanese-breakfast-pop-up-vivian-ku-today-starts-here-chinatown-los-angeles.

Star Chefs. "2021 Los Angeles Rising Star Restaurateur Vivian Ku of Joy and Pine & Crane." *Starchefs Magazine*, 2022. https://www.starchefs.com/cook/content/2021-los-angeles-rising-star-restaurateur-vivian-ku.

CHAPTER 11: FOLLOW YOUR PASSION UNAPOLOGETICALLY

Abbate, Emily. "The Real-Life Diet of Chef Daniel Humm, Who Took One of the World's Best Restaurants Vegan." *GQ,* November 18, 2021. https://www.gq.com/story/the-real-life-diet-daniel-humm.

Bruni, Frank. "A Daring Rise to the Top." *New York Times,* August 12, 2009. https://www.nytimes.com/2009/08/12/dining/reviews/12rest.html.

How I Built This with Guy Raz. "Eleven Madison Park: Daniel Humm." *How I Built This with Guy Raz,* May 3, 2021. https://www.npr.org/2021/04/28/991668793/eleven-madison-park-daniel-humm.

Star Chefs. "2005 San Francisco Rising Star Chef Daniel Humm of Campton Place—San Francisco of Campton Place." *Star Chefs Magazine.* 2005 San Francisco Rising Stars, 2022. https://www.starchefs.com/cook/chefs/rising_stars/2010/san-francisco/chef-daniel-humm.

CHAPTER 12: THE PANDEMIC

Brand, Madeleine. "How the Arts District Restaurant Bavel Managed to Survive Covid and Produce a New Cookbook." *KCRW,* June 10, 2021. https://www.kcrw.com/news/shows/press-play-with-madeleine-brand/coronavirus-economics-cryptocurrency-climate-cookbook/bavel-recipes-middle-east-hummus-covid.

Dixon, Carole. "Beverly Hills Small Businesses Are Resilient." *Beverly Hills Courier,* April 15, 2021. https://beverlyhillscourier.com/2020/10/08/beverly-hills-small-businesses-are-resilient/.

Los Angeles Magazine Staff. "An Ever-Growing List of L.A. Restaurants That Have Closed Amid the Pandemic." *Los Angeles Magazine*, January 22, 2021. https://www.lamag. com/digestblog/restaurants-closed-by-pandemic-in-los-angeles/.

Wang, Andy. "Bavel and Bestia's Culinary Power Couple Reflects on Weathering the Shutdown." *Los Angeles Magazine*, July 8, 2020. https://www.lamag.com/article/bavel-and-bestia-reopening/.

Wida, Erica Chayes. "'Real Housewives' Star Lisa Vanderpump Permanently Closes Beverly Hills Restaurant." *TODAY*, July 13, 2020. https://www.today.com/food/real-housewives-star-lisa-vanderpump-closes-beverly-hills-restaurant-t186583.

CHAPTER 13: CLOSING REMARKS: TASTE EACH BITE

Davidson, Adam. "Daniel Humm's New Eleven Madison Park Menu Will Be Meat-Free." *Wall Street Journal*, May 3, 2021. https://www.wsj.com/articles/eleven-madison-park-menu-vegan-meat-free-11620043140.

Hai Hai. "Hai Hai—Intro." Accessed January 1, 2022. https:// www.haihaimpls.com/intro.

Hatfield, Heather. "The Science behind How We Taste." WebMD, May 16, 2005. https://www.webmd.com/diet/features/science-how-we-taste#3.

BONUS CONTENT

Nichols, Chris. "How California-Born Restaurants Conquered America." *Los Angeles Magazine*, July 23, 2021. https://www. lamag.com/digestblog/california-born-restaurants/.

Thompson, Don. "California Restaurants Expect Rebound That Will Take Years." *Associated Press*, May 19, 2021. https://apnews.com/article/california-lifestyle-coronavirus-pandemic-business-health-d4deaa45439a906fcdfac2f0e12b1880.

Whitaker, Jan. "Charge It!" *Restauranting Through History*, March 25, 2016. https://restaurant-ingthroughhistory.com/2013/06/03/charge-it/.

Made in the USA
Coppell, TX
09 July 2022